HIGH GROUND

HIGH GROUND

Peak Hikes of the Mid-Atlantic States

Bill Rozday

Virgin Pines Press

Frederick, Maryland

Copyright © 1998 by Bill Rozday

Published by
VIRGIN PINES PRESS
6671 Seagull Court
Frederick, MD 21703

Interior art by Doris B. Rozday

Printed in the United States of America by Signature Printing, Gaithersburg, MD 20879.

First Edition

Library of Congress Cataloging-in-Publication Data

Rozday, Bill
    High Ground: peak hikes of the mid-Atlantic states / Bill Rozday.
      ISBN 0-9664875-0-8

                                    98-90349
                                          CIP

To my Father:
Chestnut forager of the 20's,
Ginseng hunter of the 90's,
Feet firmly on high ground.

CONTENTS

CONTENTS

LIST OF ILLUSTRATIONS

LIST OF ILLUSTRATIONS

Acknowledgements

I would like to thank a number of individuals involved with the natural history of our ridgetops and mountain crests.

Tom Hardisky, wildlife biologist, and Steve Hower, wildlife conservation officer, both with the Pennsylvania Game Commission, provided valuable information on the habits of the eastern coyote.

John Eastlake and William Spahr, foresters with the Pennsylvania Department of Environmental Resources, guided me to prime hiking areas of Pennsylvania's Black Forest.

Ann Leffel, head of the Pennsylvania chapter of the American Chestnut Foundation, patiently explained the genetic principle of botanical back-crossing.

John Peplinski, coordinator of the plant disease clinic at Penn State University, provided information on the occurrence of foxfire on the ridgetops.

Two gentlemen from the Pennsylvania Topographic and Geologic Survey went to great lengths to educate me on the geology of the ridgetops. Sam Berkheiser, Chief, Geologic Resources Division, and Bob Smith, geologist, offered insight into the importance of Tuscarora sandstone to the ridges on which we walk.

I would like to thank Cheryl Popp from Barr Enterprises, Walkersville, Maryland for efforts in preparing the manuscript.

Cover photo: View from Mount Mitchell, North Carolina

INTRODUCTION: RIDGETOPS

A few days ago, distorted from the mechanistic nature of modern life, I returned to our ridge. I had been filled with stress, taken out of myself, and that winter night, I walked along the road leading to the hilltop. My lights shone through the tree branches there as the road wound around the draw. I had known that ridge for years -- its birds, its trees.

That night, I came back into myself. The wind cracked through the branches close overhead. Ridges further away glowed dimly in the darkness as the western Pennsylvania snow came down. I walked through the sassafras trees to the light through the branches.

I learned about the nature of ridgetops 20 years ago. In my walks through the woods of the Ohio Valley, I found a certain seclusion on the moss-covered knolls situated amidst the oak forests. There, on the cushioned ground, the dense woodlands opened a bit, offering freedom from the stifling air of August and a first taste of the spring sun in March.

Even today, a particular mossy knoll comes to mind. When lumbermen cut away the local woods, they left intact that little knoll which, typical of the ridgetops, was poor in marketable

1

timber due to thin soil. They left intact not merely its trees, but all the elements of nature with which I first became acquainted and which I have never left behind.

On that ridgetop, and on all ridgetops, grow the most congenial of plants. Trailing arbutus, the pink and white wildflower with evergreen leaves, blooms there long before the person anticipating spring expects wildflowers, carrying a powerful fragrance like that of scented soap. At the close of spring, wild azalea blossoms-- again, pink; and again, fragrant--perfume the air. At all seasons, wintergreen leaves, with their teaberry scent, run along the moss.

Western Pennsylvanians know their hills as charming, lending definition to the terrain around Pittsburgh. Step back from the purely aesthetic viewpoint further into nature, however, and there appears the culture of ridges and hollows. They represent different positionings in life.

This culture of ridges and hollows further represents the relationship of an entire human era in America to its land. On the ridgetops, man continues to interact directly with the land, owing to elements of nature basically unique to these places.

My father tells me Indians roamed on the very crest of a bluff that stood above the Ohio River. Around 1920, dad and Uncle John brought toy bows and arrows to the hilltop and played with objects an ancient culture had left there. They placed arrowheads carved from stone on their bows and shot them into the surrounding forest -- white arrowheads, gray arrowheads, arrowheads of various shapes.

Those ancient people perhaps sought closeness to the sky on that knoll, closeness to the infinity from which they arose. Perhaps the location served a strategic purpose, providing a view of travelers moving up the river. My dad remembers it now -- the very crest of the bluff, the trees, the Ohio visible.

When I later moved far from the Ohio Valley, I moved by way of the ridges, to the mountains of central Pennsylvania and then the mountains of western Maryland. In central Pennsylvania, I found ridgetops that ran for mile upon mile, so far above the valleys that they created their own weather, swirling cold fog over the trailing arbutus blossoms while, in the lowlands, the spring sun shone brightly.

I found those same ridgetops in the mountains of Maryland, the same seclusion, the same elements of nature. As long as I remained on the very crests of the ridges, I felt a kind of privilege among those living things that thrived in the wind and freshness.

This book passes atop many ridges. Some bear the title "ridge" on topographic maps, while others, ridges nevertheless, never gained that title from the people who settled near them. I've named them myself. I've had a right to, a right bestowed by my interaction with their ground.

Some are remote and have known little in the manner of human activity. Some are minor in scope. In naming them, I link them to the surrounding territory and make them easy to locate. It's a privilege often exercised by outdoor travelers. By going into places that the pace of modern life causes us to neglect, we contribute to our understanding of the world.

These ridges tend to share the themes of nature I identify here, though certain ridges do highlight particular aspects. I may cite the black birch on Tussey Ridge, but I find it on Big Pine Flat Ridge as well. The elements of nature introduced here shift freely among the thousands of ridges.

Ridges vary in elevation, comprising high points of not only mountains but mere hills. In this book, they ascend in heighth. The high ground in the Mid-Atlantic region climbs upward from north to south as the Blue Ridges commence and become increasingly dominating.

This book is not an attempt to contain the entire natural history of the ridges, nor to explore them all. Rather, it is a framework for an approach to the outdoors. The ridges touch the forces of nature more than any other part of our land; I merely transfer some of that closeness. Together with their lessons in natural history, these places lend themselves to spiritual considerations with their views, their perspectives, making them places for the whole person and for all persons.

OLD BLACK LOCUST

Big Sewickley Ridge, running above the stream of the same
name, lies in the hill country behind western Pennsylvania's Ohio
River. Sewickley Creek Road leads upstream about five miles
from the town of Ambridge to the village of Pinehurst, where
Hoenig Road joins it from the left. A short distance beyond the
juncture, Cooney Hollow Road branches off to the right. Beyond
an iron bridge, a piece of rough country rises up.

This ridge lies on private property treated casually. A
woods road sometimes used by trail-bike riders leads up through
pine forest and offers an obvious path. At the ridgetop, it bears to
the left and flattens out to a slight incline. The walk ends at its
highest point, atop a knoll of sorts; at this point, about a mile into
the woods, I reverse my steps, because a housing development lies
not far ahead. The trail leads through a wooded area of perhaps a
thousand acres.

High on this ridge stands an imposing tangle of grapevines
and blackberries that I always regarded as impenetrable. At the
heart of that tangle stands the remains of a huge tree, reduced to a
woody mass, dusty within the perpetual dryness of the thicket.

I never considered that hulk of wood the source of the massive thick place until I recognized it as a black locust. Thickets like this are a characteristic of western Pennsylvania ridgetops because of the predominance of black locust there.

Endurance distinguishes the black locust. It begins by enduring the dry and poor soil of the hilltops it chooses for a home and the prevailing winds it faces every winter. Each summer, its small leaves turn brown and nearly vanish.

The stamina carries over beyond death, when the natural strength of the species keeps it standing perhaps as long as it stood while still green. Everything that happens to a dead locust suggests eventual decay, but the standing snags resist, forcing nature to bury them while erect. Moss grows on the dead wood, in particular on wood from trees growing in an east-facing situation.

The bark falls off. The tree still stands. Poison ivy, springing up in the weak ground, forms hairy trunks two inches thick and climbs all over the rocky wood, hanging down from the top like a grapevine, threatening a person's skin but never the wood itself, as it appears it should.

Age takes the side branches and drops them to the ground, but they lay there and refuse to rot, creating a maze of uneven limbs that forestall an approach to the major trunk. Bracket funguses try to draw away the material of the wood, but it doesn't fall. It begins to rot from the ground up, and then the outer shell

6

remains there like a box, sometimes charred by a brushfire that, too, has failed to remove it from the scene.

I know of a big black locust that, 20 years ago, long after it should have fallen, hosted a pair of nesting pileated woodpeckers. I am still waiting for the tree to fall. In the intervening years, logging removed most of the woodpecker habitat; again, a pair of pileateds came back to nest in that locust.

The bracket funguses on these trees stay there for 20 and 30 years, making their attempt to reduce their host to dust and clinging with a tenacity that makes them almost impossible to remove. Wanting one for a natural collectible, I waited until frost weakened the surface attaching the fungus to the bark, and then, pushing a metal bar against the brittle growth, brought it to the ground.

The fungus brackets prove hard as wood, bearing traces of moss just as the trees do. A saw cutting the back surface runs through the orange pores to expose layers that advertise each year's growth. They become so old that the upper surface sometimes crumbles, but they cling to life.

The black locust (*Robinia pseudo-acacia*) grows 40-50 feet tall on our ridgetop, though a stray specimen may reach 80 feet or more, with a trunk several feet in diameter. Most black locusts are about the diameter of a fencerail -- the potential fencerail they often represent because of the strength of their wood.

Locust wood possesses unique strength. Slam a log to the ground and it makes a ringing vibration of soundness. A locust log exasperates even a person with a chain saw. Chain saw blades wear down quickly when penetrating locust. This wood stores tremendous heat value, ranking it at the top of the list of firewoods in this aspect.

Alive, a locust trunk is marked with pronounced ridges, the bark a wintry gray color. With age, this bark loosens readily. The branches of the tree are stubby structures, unlike the long boughs of oaks or elms.

Like much that inhabits the ridgetop, the season of growth of a locust proves brief. Just beyond the peak of spring, when a touch of humidity first hints at summer, white blossoms cover the tree. They offer a strong sweetness, a counterpoint to the unchanging stoniness of a locust trunk.

Locust spreads readily. In growth habits, it resembles the sassafras, springing up in thickets and then attaining a modest size. It proves willing to colonize poor soils, which makes it an element of the ridgetop environment.

As often as not, wild grapes tangle over dead locusts, and sometimes the curled vine and orange berries of bittersweet. In a secondhand fashion, the locust creates perhaps the most important cover for wild game in western Pennsylvania. Wild grape tangles not only feed ruffed grouse but shelter them; no cover holds more of the birds, and nowhere do grapes grow more abundantly than in the locust tangles.

Gray squirrels, as well as grouse, eat wild grapes and take advantage of the concealment of their vines. Raccoons and skunks stalk these places for young birds nesting there, as well as for the fruit.

These ridgetop thickets have apparently filled such a niche since the very beginning, because the size of many locust trunks suggests original trees growing prior to the first logging. Over much of their present range, by contrast, locusts have merely sprung to life with the opening of the forest to farming.

Foresters suspect that western Pennsylvania was part of the original range of this tree, but the rapid spread of the species makes it difficult to isolate such a range. It was, however, very limited in comparison to the wide occurrence of locust today.

Twenty years ago, I witnessed the creation of a ridgetop thicket and learned part of the reason why they have persisted throughout this part of the world.

One night, an icestorm, followed by a snowstorm, struck. The flakes poured down, wetly and rapidly, accompanied by flashes of lightning. The entire forest popped and broke and cracked. The coating of ice, topped by heavy snow, attacked it and caused it to yield. The following morning, much of that forest lay strewn on the ground, impossible to walk through at a reasonable pace.

The ridgetop icestorm broke away the upper branches from an entire area of woodland. Grapevines began climbing up the treetrunks and spreading out over the broken crowns, joining into a dense roof that covered almost half an acre. Each tree trunk became a natural arbor which existed even after the death of the tree itself.

In the warmer valleys below, years of icestorms pass by as mere winter rains. The years pass, as well, without grapevine thickets. Away from the ridgetops, generations go by without the sound of grouse wings in flight.

Since this walk begins at the base of the hill, the climb proves strenuous. The footing, however, is smooth. I favor mid-April to mid-May as hiking time in southwestern Pennsylvania, because it represents a period of scarce sunny days prior to an active season of deerflies and horseflies. A second reason for hiking this path in spring is a large stand of moccasin flowers blooming beneath scrub pines halfway up the hill. For the most part, only hikers see this wild orchid, owing to the difficulty of growing it in gardens.

If possible, check with the owner before hiking on private land such as this.

The illustration is from the Ambridge, Pennsylvania 7.5-minute topographic quadrangle.

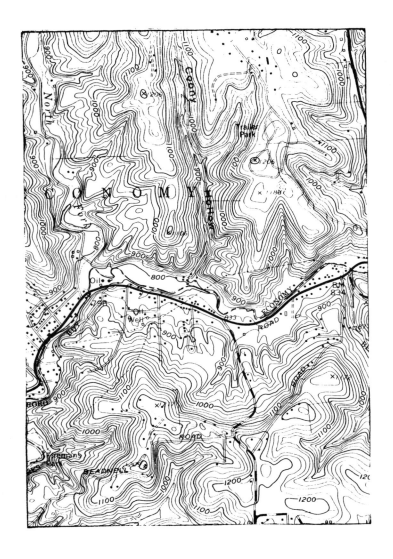

SASSAFRAS

To reach Wexford Ridge, drive the Pennsylvania Turnpike to the Interstate 79 interchange at Cranberry, then drive south on 79 to the Wexford exit. Drive on Bayne-Wexford Road to the intersection at the foot of the hill, veer right and continue right through a second intersection. Less than a mile further, the first road to the right leads to State Gamelands 203. A wide spot appears, together with a woods road leading uphill to the left. Following this, turn right at a gate and walk along the ridge. Dense sassafras dominates the woods.

On a pale ridge like this one, along a fence row where a dirt road climbed to its highest point, I remember long ago seeing then-unidentified trees, little more than shrubs, orange and yellow in autumn like the setting sun. They provided the brightest color of the countryside in October, brighter than the classic maples and poplars.

Though I grew up along that same road, I lacked a real recognition of sassafras, because that particular ridgetop stood at the very head of the Ohio River valley rather than in the true sassafras country that develops a few miles further down the river.

I developed a consciousness of sassafras when our family moved to a thin-soiled ridgetop nearer the Ohio and West Virginia borders. Then, clearing a woodlot for our home site, we encountered unfamiliar trees standing among the locusts and cherries, trees with light-colored, furrowed bark. Somehow -- perhaps we chopped into a root and caught the distinctive fragrance -- we determined them to be sassafras.

There were ridges running throughout the neighboring woods, narrow crests covered with the native forest, and I came to know sassafras further. It always grew on the crests of the ridges. There were occasional exceptions, to be sure, but only occasional. That was owing to the peculiar soil of ridgetops, which grows sassafras trees readily but other plants only with a struggle -- thin, stony soil.

On our ridgetop, I came to know sassafras intimately and recognize it for the congenial tree that it is. As I chopped away tree roots for the garden, I often struck sassafras and enjoyed the root beer fragrance.

On those occasions, I would take advantage of the opportunity to wash the roots, then shave and dry them for use in sassafras tea, a classic natural beverage. Boiling water over the roots produces a red tea with a distinct, pleasant flavor.

My paternal grandmother used sassafras. She marketed bootleg whisky in the hollow below the ridgetop of my childhood. Her Prohibition-era product found ready buyers because of its distinct appearance. She took sassafras and dropped it into the bottle before capping it, turning the whisky red.

I learned the scent of sassafras leaves, then found the different scent of the limbs -- both pleasant, though not as strong as that of the roots. The tree even gave us yellow blossoms in the springtime.

Sassafras flowers late in spring, carrying out the theme of the lengthened winter on the ridgetops. By the time the lemon-yellow flowers appear in May, only four months remain before the birches and black gums drop their leaves.

Sassafras has penetrated American culture more so than perhaps any other tree. The distinctive fragrance and flavor of the roots have appeared in various products, from root beer to the scented soap I recently purchased from a crafts store in West Virginia. Sassafras has been a recognizable presence for hundreds of years. In the early days of America, the roots proved a valuable item of export. The definitive scent and flavor convinced many that they possessed medicinal power.

Sassafras (*Sassafras albidum*) has a botanical uniqueness. Only three members of the sassafras family exist on earth, one of the other two in Asia and another on the island of Formosa. In America, it occurs widely, from Maine to Florida and west to Michigan and Texas.

The tree also bears structural peculiarities. Three types of leaves occur on each tree: one-lobed, two-lobed, and three-lobed.

The seasonal cycle of the tree proceeds through the flowers to tiny, berry-like fruits of a blue color. Birds of various species esteem them; they constitute valuable food because of the free distribution of the species.

Young sassafras trees appear brownish-green, but this changes to a grayish-brown as the tree ages. Furrows develop in the bark and become deep, producing a wrinkled appearance. The tree averages perhaps 30 feet tall, through in the sassafras country of my earlier days, it reaches 80 and sometimes becomes 2 feet in diameter. The wood itself finds random use in fenceposts and walking sticks, but as true lumber, it proves weak and brittle, fulfilling its highest purpose in boxmaking or boatbuilding.

Yet, other sassafras products continue to find a ready market. Supermarkets often carry packets of sassafras root bark for use in tea. For those in sassafras country who do not sell the bark directly to grocery stores, firms dealing in botanicals circulate lists of prices offered per pound of bark harvested.

It was a poor tree, a plant of rough places, but it offered itself freely and displayed many virtues. In the autumn, it provided two colors: an occasional ruby-red, and a familiar rich orange-yellow. Sassafras foliage turns color with an exceptional vividness.

The little sassafras trees I saw when young remind me that no matter how degraded or scarred or rocky the environment, sassafras will spring forth. It parallels our lives. This is hardly a stately tree, like the redwoods or firs of the West. Yet, it is a tree close to the people -- and destined to remain so. Stately trees such as those of the West need special protection to spare them from destruction, and the very laws that protect them are made to be broken.

I came to relish the peculiar familiarity with sassafras that living on the ridgetop gave. Visitors looked blankly at the sassafrasses in the yard, unable to identify them. When a windstorm swept over the ridge and uprooted a large tree from the weak soil, I gathered great quantities of tea bark from large roots.

I even came to know sassafras wood. Lightning aided my knowledge when it struck two large specimens on the ridge. I picked up a long shaft of the wood, split without my efforts, and used it as a ready-made fence rail.

My father recently cut up the thick trunk of one that had fallen, leaving a stump that showed fifty years of growth. It had grown just over the edge of the ridge, a tedious walk to the woodpile but an invitation to physical labor.

In the Ohio Valley rain, I set to work carrying the wood. Neither aspen-light nor locust-heavy, the large chunks nevertheless approached 100 pounds in weight.

In an earlier day, books often carried tables indicating which firewoods possessed certain qualities of fragrance, heat, and lasting power. I encountered one of those recently in a book published in 1910, Horace Kephart's classic "The Book of Camping and Woodcraft."

The author cites several woods easily obtained on ridgetops, sour gum, sassafras, and pitch pine, as nearly inflammable while green. Sassafras, fortunately, is often found in a cured state, owing to its durability after falling.

My Ohio Valley sassafras wood split with greater ease than any wood I've known, like a breaking rock. It burnt with energy and more than sufficient heat. The smoke perfuming the fireplace extended the pattern of fragrance and, in this continuity, expressed the character of nature.

Those who burn conifer know how it smokes and cracks, but only a few who are familiar with the ridges know the entertaining sounds of sassafras wood. It crackles and crackles -- lives with ridgetop spirit and then burns with it.

This path offers a wide surface for walking and an easy-to-follow route, but I recommend it prior to the deerfly season, which commences in mid-May. Again, in autumn, the hunters on this Game Commission property make wearing orange garments advisable. In the days leading up to deer season at the end of November, a nearby shooting range creates a great deal of noise as hunters practice shooting for the approaching season.

The illustration is from the Mars, Pennsylvania 7.5-minute topographic quadrangle.

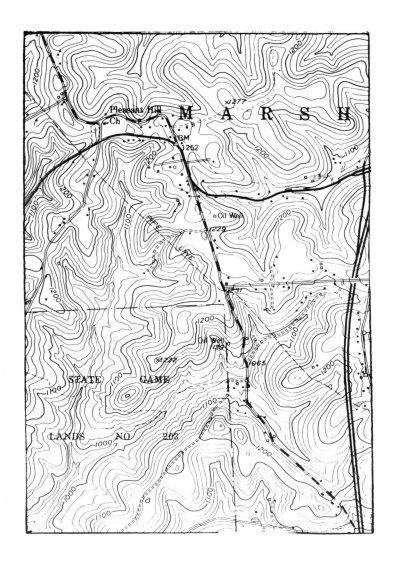

BRIGHT RIDGES

This hike follows the Appalachian Trail behind Caledonia State Park, on the boundary of Pennsylvania's Franklin and Adams Counties. Route 233 leads beyond the park to the first side road branching left. Though paved at first, the road becomes dirt and dead-ends on the ridge. A short walk to the left, the Appalachian Trail appears in the midst of its route to Georgia.

This ridge hosts the distinctive trees and plants that bring color to the mid-Atlantic ridges, the birches, the ferns, even the trunks of the old chestnuts, killed by blight.

It reminds me of an ancient chestnut split apart long-wise, a melon of red dust, across a shale pit and into the ridgetop woods in western Pennsylvania. That treetrunk symbolized the history of my ridges. Perhaps the largest in the entire vicinity, it lent identity to that patch of ground.

Near that chestnut log was a second distinctive tree, this one standing. It was bright and shiny in appearance, as though the dryness and sterility of the ridgetop had produced a fresh and gleaming treetrunk almost metallic, beyond the decay around it. It was as though the trunk was sheathed in flame. No other tree of its kind existed in the area.

They called it fire cherry. In the name, I saw its bright color. I also came to understand the relation of the name to the tree's habit of following forest fires in its occurrence. During the days when I first explored that section of woods, one of the forest fires that tend to favor ridgetops burned the ground and lower trees there, spreading an unusual scent of burning growth through the May night.

Later, I came to know the broad mountaintops of the Appalachian chain. There, stands of fire cherry existed as an element. Its color remained throughout the winter, in the pure sun, gleaming like copper in the hardness of the mountain environment, together with the silver of the snow.

Fire cherry (*Prunus pensylvanica*) is also known as pin cherry or bird cherry. It is considered a small tree, averaging perhaps 25 feet in height and seldom reaching a foot in diameter. Its leaves and flowers resemble those of the standard cherry tree. The fruits, though tart to our taste, feed ruffed grouse, while deer browse on the branches. Fire cherry thereby contributes to the furtherance of wildlife in the secluded and neglected environments which, by their very nature, afford opportunities for wildlife. This species occurs over a wide range, from British Columbia across to Newfoundland, south to Colorado and Pennsylvania and then, in the mountains, all the way to Georgia and Tennessee.

The fire cherry is part of a brightness that characterizes ridgetops. Because of their pattern of abundance, the trees typical of the ridges produce general schemes of color that exist in all seasons. I noted that brightness one late winter day.

At strong odds with the gray of the valley trees, a thicket of branches glowed red-orange -- a stand of striped maples amidst the perpetual green of mountain laurel, the branches a tangle of sunset color. The branches attain these bright hues as the sap rises in them with the approach of spring.

Striped maple, or moosewood (*Acer pensylvanicum*) stands perhaps 20 feet tall. White stripes run along its bark. It grows from Nova Scotia to Manitoba, south to Pennsylvania and Ohio and further south in the mountains to Tennessee and Georgia.

The trees that brighten the ridgetops are not imposing in their dimensions. Like striped maple, sour gum (*Nyssa sylvatica*) is a small tree, with minor exceptions. It stands perhaps 50 feet tall, its bark broken into tiny squares and grooved deeply. The leaves have a leathery texture. As does fire cherry, sour gum feeds ruffed grouse with its fruit, and wild turkey as well. It ranges from Maine across to Michigan and Missouri, south to Texas and Florida, but it grows with particular energy on Caledonia Ridge.

Ridgetops display a color scheme unique to them. In August, while the katydids sing in green woods and vacationers lay on the white sand of the mountain lakes, the ridgetops begin to gleam with the sunset color of turning sour gum leaves. Autumn passes over the sour gums unknown to those who do not frequent the ridges or know the types of trees there. In the valleys, more than a month will pass before attention is given to a turning leaf.

A second time before autumn makes itself known elsewhere, it shines on the ridge. Entire thickets of sweet birch turn bright lemon in September. Then comes their coal-gray of leaf absence, before most autumn color in the forest commences.

On the September ground, sarsaparilla plants turn yellow and fade away. Virginia creeper leaves dyed red-pink run over the stones. The last of the goldenrod standing amidst those rocks dies. In the narrowness of the ridgetop autumn, hayscented ferns, their fronds bronze, breathe a coconut-like fragrance.

Well-defined and limited, as are the ridgetops, the seasons of the crests pass with a rugged brightness.

I recommend this hike on a summer day because of the various facilities near to it. At Caledonia State Park is a campground. The adjacent acreage offers picnicking and swimming, as well as fishing.

The illustration is from the Caledonia Park, Pennsylvania 7.5-minute topographic quadrangle.

HAWKS

To reach Kittatinny Ridge, follow route 81 south to Pennsylvania 61 at Hamburg. Route 895 then leads north to Drehersville, close to the sanctuary.

Kittatinny Ridge, on which Hawk Mountain lies, offers a hiking experience more formal than most. Access to the trails comes with a fee -- $4.00 per day. Near the trail gate stands a large parking lot, complete with attendant.

The trail follows the ridge for a considerable distance, but all of this ground falls within the domain of the staff naturalists, who interpret it heavily in person, ranging along the paths at peak visitation times. The ridge carries an unusual number of hikers and nature-lovers. They feel cared-for here, which they are.

Kittatinny Ridge shows how, once a way into the outdoors becomes apparent, it leads on for a certain distance. Beyond delving into the nature of ridgetops, I found myself gravitating toward specific points of high country. In much the same way, reading a book on ridgetops begins a personal pursuit of them. Given sufficient time in natural settings, entire approaches to the outdoors suggest themselves. Only the lack of time limits this re-creation of our relationship to the land.

In our country today, our limited time outdoors tends toward the ridges. They constitute a significant aspect of the outdoors experience for the person restricted to vacation time or weekends.

Skyline Drive and the Blue Ridge Parkway, the most famous drives in the east, consist essentially of a ridgetop ride for nearly 550 miles. I chanced to drive the Blue Ridge Parkway this spring, finding that it carried forth my understanding of the ridges.

The brushy trees I had noted on gypsy-moth-ridden oak ridges of Pennsylvania were encouraged in their growth by Indians of the Blue Ridges. They burnt the ridgetops in order to force their growth. The dense brush attracted game animals in numbers. The Indians essentially created hunting grounds in this manner. Realizing this reminds me that man's relationship with the ridges is one of our primary interactions with nature.

A casual drive earlier in the season led to a Pennsylvania hilltop on which stood a virtual ghost town -- the town of Centralia, evacuated because of an underground coal mine fire.

The highway becomes abandoned here, a gate thrown across it. The hike leads down the middle of the highway, where the fire, burning now for 35 years, sends up a sulfurous smell for great distances. Warm steam issues forth from alongside rocks, or from cracks in the road's asphalt. Dead oak trees, destroyed by these conditions, stand along with the brushy sassafras.

Beyond this demonstration of ludicrous land management, a long ridge sweeps over the horizon. A church stands nearby, deserted, silent as the cemetery behind it. A pathway climbs to the highest point, windy and cold that day. Against the grayness stand gray birches, the tree of rough ground, their trunks pale.

This ridge is a symbol of bleakness. The fiery destruction beneath it reflects the destruction of the entire coal industry of northeastern Pennsylvania. A heart of emptiness exists here.

Another weekend brought me to Tuscarora Ridge, 2100 feet high, one of the south-central Pennsylvania ridgetops. The Tuscarora Trail runs over it, like many hiking trails that follow the high places. I walked along, watching for trailing arbutus blossoms and coming upon a stand of white birches, the most southerly I had ever encountered.

The ridgetop settings tend to be highly visible. At a popular Pennsylvania state park, Pine Grove Furnace, a trail leads to a well-known rock formation, the Pole Steeple. The path climbs to the top of a ridge where, far back in the surrounding forest, people sit on rock perches as they might on a beach, absorbing the sense of space and perspective. Others climb the rocks with ropes.

One of the famous ridges of the Appalachians is Hawk Mountain Sanctuary, on Kittatinny Ridge. Those who created the sanctuary in 1934, as well as the thousands who visited it this past year, did so in recognition of the interplay of wind and this particular ridgetop. This interplay brings the path of thousands of migrating hawks along the fringe of the ridge.

Beth and I stepped from among the sweet birch and chestnut oak to one of the rock fields on the crest. In short order, a small hawk flitted by, almost too quickly to follow with the binoculars. The Indian summer sun shone on our perch as hawks occasionally swept past, traveling at 40 miles per hour.

Thermal currents, rising from the action of warming sun on the ridge, direct the hawks in a line conforming to that of the crest itself. Prevailing winds strike the ridge, which diverts the air currents upward and provides a further guiding effect. This track of flight brings the birds to within yards of the hundreds of people observing on a suitable day, one with a northerly or westerly prevailing wind.

On our trip to Hawk Mountain, we visited the peak of a season as well as of a ridge. On that day, sharp-shinned hawks dominated as a species, as they typically do at that time of year. October 14th actually became a record-setting day for sharp-shin sightings. A northwest wind pushed the sailing hawks close to the portion of the crest on which we took up a perch. Earlier, in September, broad-winged hawks represent the most common species.

Along the paths, a steady stream of people walked with their families. The sun shone through the gold of witchhazel leaves, with the accompanying gold of their flowers. From the rock outcroppings, mountain ash foliage shone gold as well, together with its clusters of red berries. The warmth brought forth katydids to sing among the trees.

Someday, Hawk Mountain will not contain all of the people striving to rise above the triviality of our society to consider elemental matters. They crowd into a visitor's center to purchase nature books or bird feeders, occupy each stray rock on the ridgetop. A small proportion of people, they will nevertheless increase. Their enthusiasm and knowledge prove as unique as the wind on this ridge. This place represents a significant crest in the cultural sense.

On ridges such as Hawk Mountain, we recover perspective and approach long-lost days of abundance. We look at these hawks glide by just as the years have glided by. Only 63 years have passed since market gunners shot hawks from the top of this mountain. Their interaction with nature was cruel, if intimate in its directness.

As the years pass, we move further beyond such a primitive conception of nature, yet with our binoculars and guidebooks and studies of wind currents, we yearn for that quality of life we see less and less of but that the market gunners knew, the quality of abundance, here perceived riding on these wind currents and on the grays and browns and whites of the hawks.

Hawk Mountain provides an example of restricted interaction with nature. Here, we approach the edge of the rich relationship with nature our forefathers enjoyed, but we merely study and reflect. The owners of the ridgetop designate this a sanctuary, which prohibits any real use of the forest resources other than by wildlife.

Ridgetops vary in this relationship to man in accordance with who owns them. I know of many electric powerline right-of-way roads running over hilltops and offering convenient parking and free range to passersby. Many ridgetops affording scenic views tend to feature pulloffs.

The Blue Ridge Parkway provides a less-regulated experience than does Hawk Mountain. Not only does the Parkway permit parking on the grassy shoulder of the road, but short walks from the road often lead to National Forest property. The government manages National Forests with a view toward extensive resources such as timber, giving the average berry-picker or mushroom-hunter a carefree day unmarred by rules.

I also find a loose approach in Pennsylvania's State Forests. Like the National Forests, their acreage proves so great that restrictions are unnecessary and impractical. This holds true to a varying degree in State Forests of other states.

Another of man 's institutions within the nature of the ridges is the Appalachian Trail. This path employs the crest of the Appalachians, the crest representing their defining feature. This placement of the trail also removes it from the disturbances typical of low country.

HAWKS

Hikers and backpackers interact with nature in more direct ways than casual walkers parking at overlooks. They also walk far from roads, our connection to the regulation of civilized life. Therefore, they encounter no signs warning against the consumption of natural resources. Their transient nature ensures against most abuse of such.

Traveling from one ridge to another constitutes an education in natural history, but remaining on a single ridge, watching the seasons and years pass over it, offers its own education, a deeper understanding. Another of the truths of our relationship to nature is the ability of a given piece of land to show us, given sufficient time, the same things that ridgetops traveled to show us.

Like a human life, my ridge back home houses the seeds of various endeavors, accomplishments; and it presents objects of interest -- given time. I returned there in mid-May, to Amsler Ridge Road, Sewickley, Pennsylvania.

A near-unprecedented cold spell moved over the hilltop during my stay -- snow pellets in May. Excessive rain had fallen during the entire season. I found myself walking among the dead elms in the woodlands there.

I found a large morel mushroom (*Morchella esculenta*) and, upon noting several others, recognized a positive contribution that the heavy rainfall had made. I saw morel mushrooms on the woodland floor in places that had never featured them before -- at least in 25 years. Walking along the road, I spotted one standing on the grassy bank; stepping beyond it under the elms, I saw an entire patch of large morels, the finest I have ever known -- a hundred yards from the house.

Each day away from my ridge has been a day of rain, because I know that ridge. I not only see it, but I know it, and this type of knowing, coming about from the depths of our perceptions, from a fixed point traveled over by change, we all seek; away from what we know, we feel lost.

My ridge has brought me a deep comfort, yet a hard realization when away from it. This absolute love, this knowledge, each life finds, and that fact sustains my steps on the ridge.

Route 81 leads to other ridges of interest in this area. The ridge at Centralia, site of the long-burning coal fire, also lies along Route 61, north from 81. A sign at the town of Ashland indicates the associated road closure a short distance up the hill.

Pine Grove Furnace State Park, with its Pole Steeple, is situated near Shippensburg, south of Harrisburg. Exit 11 off of 81 leads along Route 233 directly to the park. A left turn and several miles bring Laurel Lake. The first dirt road below the lake follows it along the base of the mountain to a parking lot for the trail.

Tuscarora Ridge, from which Tuscarora sandstone receives its name, runs above Cowans Gap State Park, reached from Exit 6 off of 81, then Route 30 and Route 75. Turnoffs beside transmission towers on the ridge provide parking.

Whereas the walk at Centralia merely follows the center of a highway, the hike at Hawk Mountain proves rocky enough to demand leather shoes. The trail to the Pole Steeple involves an uphill hike culminating in a difficult climb into a break within the rocks, but the strenuous portion only consumes a few moments.

Both Hawk Mountain and the Pole Steeple present views impressive enough to prove worthwhile at any time during the warm months. I favor mountain laurel season, May, for both, though Hawk Mountain's birdwatching makes September and October favored months.

The illustration is from the New Ringgold, Pennsylvania 7.5-minute topographic quadrangle.

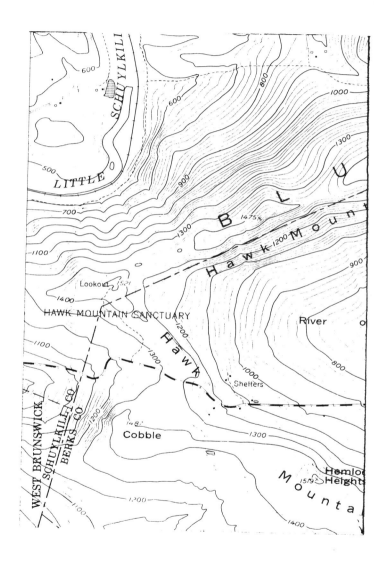

BRACKET FUNGUSES

The road into the heart of Maryland's Catoctin Mountains, Route 77, turns left beyond the federal government's visitor center and becomes Catoctin Hollow Road. On the right, at the lower end of Hunting Creek Lake, look for a parking lot. Across the road from the lot, a trail leads onto Cat Rock Ridge.

Further up Catoctin Hollow Road, about half a mile beyond the entrance to Cunningham Falls State Park, the Catoctin Trail leads onto the same ridge. Parking here is limited to a few pulloffs, unmarked.

This ridge illustrates how, on the crests, nature's strongest weather battles nature's strongest trees. During the struggle, many an oak falls. The forces of weather ally themselves with gypsy moth and fungal infestations, which find targets in the species of trees that frequent high elevations. After killing the trees, the moth onslaught leaves them standing, but prone to infestations of Armillaria, or shoestring fungus, which works to weaken their lower portions. The storms attack the oaks in their debilitated state, causing widespread destruction in the forests.

The storms are often icestorms. Striking the ridgecrest, they break trees in half, leaving them shorn stubs, bending living branches double, their faces on the earth, cracking branches and depositing them everywhere. Icestorms are storms of elevation, felling trees past a certain altitude, below which harmless rain falls.

A major tree, perhaps the single most important tree of the ridgecrests, is chestnut oak. On the crests, its trunk takes on the green of lichens, which make it appear something other than wood. The hardness of the trunk, together with the clean atmosphere in which it rises up, provide an ideal setting for the lichens, which adopt the wood as if it were stone. Chestnut oak wood has perhaps been an element of ridgecrests for ages and ages, judging by the way lichens find their way to the furrowed trunks, as they do to the rock surfaces on the ground.

Chestnut oak (*Quercus prinus*) is certainly an Appalachian tree, limited in its distribution to regions near to the mountain chain. Rock oak is a nickname. It occurs from the very southern tip of Maine south to Alabama and west as far as Mississippi.

This is typically the largest tree of the ridgetops, though it generally grows only 60 or so feet tall. It develops a thicker trunk, certainly, than the average birch or sassafras. The trunk is blocked off with distinct ridges, the bark a coal-gray color.

This tree gains its name from the shape of its leaves, very much like that of the American chestnut. The edges are a bit more round, however, and the length less.

The oaks of the ridgetops, dying from gypsy moth and Armillaria attack, feature on their trunks a symbolic indication of struggle: bracket funguses that remain for years and attain large proportions. I once salvaged one close to two feet across, a chalky-white specimen I pried away with a tire iron.

This bracket fungus is a type with the scientific name *Ganoderma applanatum*, but more pale than the typical brown of that species. This whitish variation proves common throughout much of the Appalachians because the types of trees it associates with -- oak, chiefly -- prove the most common trees. They comprise almost the entire forest on many ridges and, as the largest trees, offer a generous setting of trunk for the fungus to dwell upon. Its size and abundance, together with its fresh appearance, make this species of bracket fungus a popular craft material, the smooth underside used for painting.

This Appalachian craft possesses a long history. I know of a fungus painting over 60 years old, preserved with varnish and in perfect condition, the material having taken on the qualities of wood and resisted decay.

The use of bracket funguses for painting has justification. They represent, in a sense, slices of life. Their position within the context of the outdoors supports their use as a medium for illustrations of nature. I envision artists celebrating days outdoors by painting the scenic views opening up from the location of the fungus and its treetrunk.

This is an art form of the mountains, and of America, a product of the uncivilized settings of the New World. It is the highlands of our country that possess the forest cover that produces these growths, together with the humid climate, and the life force which finds expression in fungus painting.

Coastal artists often paint on wave-smoothed fragments of ship boards, but man fashioned such material once before it was torn apart and offered up by the waves. On the ridgetops, artists paint upon the pure surge of life from treetrunks reaching for the sky.

The ruining of the ridgetop forest by the elements forces expressions of reclamation from nature -- varying expressions. Trees such as red maple, sweet birch, sassafras, and aspen often crowd the earth in an effort to supplant the lost oaks. Pitch pine and mountain pine break the wind, causing it to sigh as it passes. As much a component of such thickets as the trees themselves is the ruffed grouse, perhaps the finest of all gamebirds.

On the ridge that runs above the Allegheny River, the quaking aspen (*Populus tremuloides*) that grows there drops heaps of its weak branches onto the ground, producing excellent grouse cover. In autumn, the gold color of aspen foliage on ridges throughout western Pennsylvania proves a grouse hunting guide.

Ridgecrests bring the northern quaking aspen south with them, where, in the Appalachians, the aspen meets sweet birch (*Betula lenta*). This birch has a limited range as compared to that of other birches. It extends no further westward from the mountains than Ohio, also remaining close to the Appalachians as it runs southward into northern Georgia and Alabama.

Black birch is also known as cherry birch. It bears oval, toothed leaves similar to those of a cherry, and tight bark of a hue also suggestive of that tree. Wild black cherry (*Prunus serotina*) resembles black birch strongly, the similarity so great that it forces the test of breaking a twig from each and smelling it. Black birch bears a distinct wintergreen fragrance.

The ridgetops also feature a unique form of tree -- a miniature oak. Known as bear oak (*Quercus ilicifolia*), it resembles the oak trees that accompany it in the high places, but it stands only around 10 feet high. These miniature oaks are limited in every sense: they offer no firewood, little shade, little food for wildlife, at least as individual trees. It is as if the struggle of all life on the ridges takes concrete form in the abbreviated nature of these oaks.

The small size of bear oak leaves, more elm-sized than oak-sized, distinguishes them. Their trunks, only a couple of inches in diameter, suggest those of a gentler tree, perhaps a serviceberry.

Bear oak grows in abundance, and it offers an abundance of color in autumn. The distinctive tones of the trees serve adequately to identify them, because they look nothing like the yellow of the chestnut oak foliage that often accompanies them.

The foliage of these miniature oaks turns an acorn color. It is a warm mixture of hues, not entirely acorn-brown, but with glows of red, orange, yellow -- an intimate blending of color, not the crayon hues of maples, but an artist's colors.

Oak color makes the ridgetops a private preserve of aesthetics in autumn, because it arrives after the customary period of leaf-watching. This year, it came in the first week of November at the northern end of the Blue Ridges. Entire crests of chestnut oak stood pheasant-gold in the rain.

At the break of spring, the snow disappears last from the patches of hayscented fern that spring up in the fresh sun admitted with the dying of the oaks. The deer of the thickets walk into the openness of the fern patches like shadows in the twilight, tails white like snow, fleeing through the open as they would never do in daylight.

In early spring, the only sound on the ridgetops is wind in the pine boughs. Under the oaks lie the brown leaves, the winter struggle above them completed.

The struggle gives us deer to hunt, grouse to hunt, bracket funguses to hunt. It gives us an increasing abundance that is rare in an era of overuse.

The Catoctins, situated in Maryland, benefit from a sunny summer, which provides pleasant hiking. However, a mild day in winter offers the aesthetics of sunlight on the forest limbs and trunks. Aside from flowers and leaves, everything visible in summer is equally visible in winter. Furthermore, the willingness to hike in all seasons brings the outdoors completely to a person and allows it to satisfy him or her fully.

The illustration is from the Catoctin Furnace, Maryland 7.5-minute topographic quadrangle.

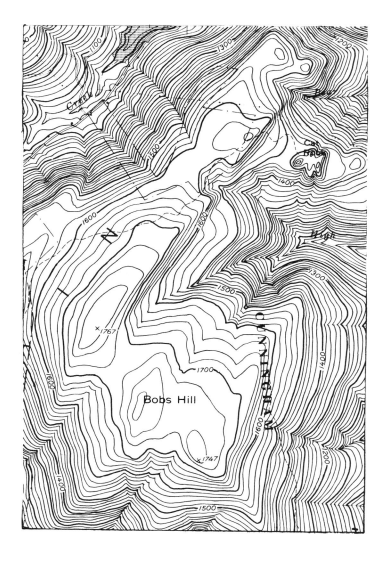

BRUSH WOLVES

Peters Ridge lies in a neglected piece of country not far from Interstate 81 in eastern Pennsylvania. From exit 33, Route 209 leads west to Tower City, near the boundary of Dauphin and Schuykill Counties. From there, Route 325, actually 10th Street, runs westward out of town until it reaches an intersection. At a sign for Goldmine Road, turn right. Continue on, bearing left onto Greenland Road, which leads to State Gamelands 210.

Follow the road uphill until, well toward the top, a small parking lot appears on the right and a woods road leads into the forest. This area offers many miles of hiking in undisturbed territory, with the security of a definite route to follow and light use, owing to the area's management for hunting. It contains over 11,000 acres of land, together with 20 miles of lightly-used roads.

This ridge affords the opportunity to confirm the existence of a wilderness symbol -- the wolf. Such symbols prove difficult to authenticate, because their status as wilderness creatures embodies a certain elusiveness. When and how they become established, or vanish, only they themselves know.

In rugged Tioga County, Pennsylvania, in 1942, only a few decades after the last wolf in Pennsylvania supposedly died, a wolf-like animal appeared, increasing its numbers in coming years. Perhaps some quality of environment, some extreme protectiveness of landscape, preserved it. Perhaps it was driven to such a place; then, following the logging era, stepped forth. Perhaps, after these animals disappear once more, they will emerge anew, from Tioga County.

The wolf, then, never vanished with finality from these hilltops. Today, scientists affirm its presence through modern studies. They refer to the animal as the eastern coyote. The wolf-like coyotes we see today carry 15 percent gray wolf genes. A defining tendency of the wolf, that of running in packs, is also apparent.

Today's wolves come from the interbreeding of western coyotes and gray wolves. The issue of naming -- wolf or coyote -- turns on the question of whether the settlers' wolves in early Pennsylvania carried 15 percent wolf genes, as ours, or represented animals with pure wolf constitutions. One expert on the animal, Steve Hower, tells of a settler's "wolf" preserved at Cornell University which, when analyzed, proved basically identical to the animals of today. Hunters refer to our animals as "brush wolves."

The eastern coyote (*Canis latrans*) possesses more than enough size and weight to be seen commonly in the wild, did its secretive nature not prevent this. The animal's length ranges from 4-5 feet. It weighs 35-50 pounds. The color of the eastern coyote varies -- white, tan, gray, black, though a typical coyote is gray with tan and reddish, broken by black vertical lines in the legs. Coyote eyes are generally yellow.

In mid-April to early May, around 6 pups are born; they begin to leave the family group by October. They travel 30-50 miles from their place of birth, which explains how the population of coyotes builds rapidly. In 20 years, the population in Pennsylvania went from 100 to 10,000.

Coyotes eat plant and fruit material, but they concentrate their hunting efforts on rodents and small mammals. Insects and birds form some portion of the diet, but deer meat from a variety of sources is the most widely consumed item, whether from roadkills, deer dead from starvation; or occasionally, fawns hunted down. The coyote possesses the capability to kill sheep, goats, chickens, cats and dogs.

Coyotes fall victim to guns, generally during hunting season when spotted incidental to deer or bear. Conscious efforts to trap or hunt them account for perhaps 2000 animals a year in Pennsylvania.

Biologists debate whether Pennsylvania's animals migrated from the more open country to the north or merely survived unnoticed. The fact remains that the wolf lives on in those genes, that the wilderness resurges on the ridges.

Eighty years ago, the single transaction of these ridges with man -- lumbering -- ended. The high places stood there. In the face of the weather, their heights captured the rain. Trees grew, filling in a wilderness of space and silence remaining. The origin of wolves was this silence, and their resurgence proceeds largely in secret, leaving signs but few sightings of the animal itself. We know only what we see and record today.

They told me they ran the ridgetop at night -- along firelanes, because ridges feature firelanes built to gain perspective on forest fires climbing the mountainsides. These lanes also provide brushy openings where the small creatures that wolves prey upon live.

The coyote range I visited in eastern Pennsylvania consisted of scarred land from which man had recently faded away. Against the long and straight lines of ridges, the open blackness of abandoned coal mines runs. The land struggles to recover itself after the long-ago abuses of lumbering, bringing forth modest oaks and sassafrasses, fire cherry with sooty-looking trunks the color of coal that change, in sunlight, to the reddish color of coal burning in shadows. "Forest" is too refined a designation for this wolf country for one who has seen Pennsylvania's Black Forest, or North Carolina's Black Mountains.

In the crisp air of a February day, morning sun working through the scrubby oaks backing the snow-covered line of a woods road, I walked along with a like-minded friend curious about coyotes. We saw the fragile mark of a mouse crossing from the laurel and huckleberry to the laurel and huckleberry across the white road. There ran a skunk's feet in the previous night's snow.

Flowing out of the winter shrubs as naturally as mountain air, rather than in a dog's domestic way, came a straight line of prints that carried authority. Their solidity and definitiveness arrested us. They came from a coyote. Down the woods road they went, to where a second set joined them. A grouse burst out from the fringes, leaving a complex network of bird track behind.

Those tracks ran across our trail because of the helpfulness of a coyote specialist, Tom Hardisky, who directed me to the border area of Dauphin and Schuykill Counties and suggested I visit during January or February, the animals' mating season. They further originated in the efforts of Steve Hower, who guided me to this particular mountaintop; and Joe Kosack, who remarked on the coyote's propensity for woods roads.

The tracks broke away from the woods lane into the laurel as we also did, and our hunting instincts filtered through the forest branches, supplanting the spoken advice that introduced us to the animals and that remained in our minds. The tree boughs and shrubs led to the brow of the ridge at a point where the tracks descended into a fold of land sheltered from the wind.

Upon seeing a formation of rock ahead in an area largely devoid of stone, I approached it. We looked at coyote tracks entering a bit of a tunnel formed by rock lying at an angle. Sean peered in and saw, in a deposit of old leaves, the flattened bed of a coyote. At a second rock formation, tracks led to an impenetrable cavity.

We followed coyote tracks back to the woods road and speculated on the whereabouts of the animals -- miles away, perhaps. We needed to leave the ridge, so we also speculated on how close the den in the rocks brought us to a future sighting of a coyote itself, since we knew the animals used more than one den.

The den made the coyote a less unstable presence, holding the animal in one place rather than it roaming over its 25 square miles of range. The animal considered those rocks an undisturbed location -- and so it is, without a covering of snow to tie a set of tracks to it. Coyotes will likely revisit the site.

Americans have always retained a certain distance from their land. We truly knew it little more in the 1800s than the 1990s. In an era of regimentation and environmental destruction, the resurgence of a wild and secretive animal points out how the ridges function as something of a land beyond. Walk the mountaintops and pay respects to the independent strength of the wolf. Take pictures of tracks and dens. What we know of the animal begins anew now, and begins with us.

The light use of Game Commission property in periods between hunting seasons makes a hike such as this an opportunity to move within the season of summer without distractions, to know the signs of those months fully. The lack of hunters also encourages coyotes to move about more freely, providing the possibility of spotting one. By autumn, hunters dominate this area; winter in this part of the mid-Atlantic proves harsh.

47

The illustration is from the Tower City, Pennsylvania 7.5-minute topographic quadrangle.

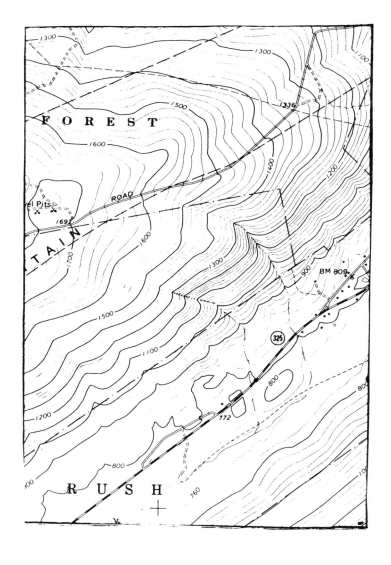

49

GINSENG

Foxville Ridge marks a high point of the Catoctin Mountains, a popular and easy-to-reach area in western Maryland. Route 15, running south from Harrisburg, Pennsylvania, meets Route 77 at Thurmont, Maryland. A left turn at the end of the exit leads uphill for several miles to a road running left, which leads in turn to the entrance to Cunningham Falls State Park. Inside the gate to the park, the road ends in a large parking lot and in-season fee station. Across the beach to the left and into the woods, signs point toward Cunningham Falls. Once on the ridge, the trail intersects the longer Catoctin Trail.

Before I camped on Foxville Ridge, I had never found ginseng on the ridgetop before. It had always seemed to grow in the deep hollows, near waterfalls and wildflower-covered boulders, in coolness and freshness. I knew the ridgetops as dry and hard, not a place for delicate life such as ginseng, the most celebrated of American plants.

Where it grows on that ridgetop in the Catoctins of Maryland, the light from a polished moon fell on the leaves and forest plants last night. This morning, tawny patches of sunlight replaced the moonglow. With spicewoods shadowing it, then the straight and tall trunks of maple and ash, it stood at the foot of a

50

jumble of boulders jutting from the crest; the plants it so often associates with standing there as well: black cohosh, wild ginger.

I knew why it grew here. Ginseng digging had driven it uphill, and inward -- miles into the woods, far above the sun-soaked valley leading to Washington, in the night, the lights of people twinkling far below, miles away, through a break in the mountains near their highest crest.

Seeing the ginseng, a small bed of it, took my mind away. I wondered about it, wondered how much grew there. Ginseng hunting, though, takes the mind too far away, to places that are not real today. Ginseng is a hint, a fleck of old times, the past.

Ginseng (*Panax quinquefolius*), as guidebooks to wildflowers tell us, grows 12-18 inches tall on average. The range encompasses Ontario south to Georgia, including most of the Eastern states. The leaf stem forks in three or four directions; at the end of each fork grow five leaves arranged like fingers radiating from a hand. At the forking of the main stem stands a pale flower which, toward autumn, becomes a group of red berries.

The root of the ginseng plant, like the stem, forks off. These forks give the appearance of arms and legs. At the point closest to the ground surface, a knotty extension of the root runs along, bearing scars marking each year of the plant's life.

Americans have known ginseng for over two centuries, throughout that time digging ginseng roots in autumn and selling them to buyers who in turn ship them to the Orient.

A large patch of ginseng translated into considerable wealth in the early days. A large patch of ginseng translates into considerable wealth today, but such occurrences of the plant prove more hypothetical than practical.

Twenty years ago, I dug and marketed a tiny amount of ginseng at the rate of $90 per dried pound. In 1995, the price reached $400. About 150 roots equal a pound -- and typically, several weeks worth of hunting and digging.

I wanted to find more ginseng in the woods where it grew. We stepped into the trees with the intent of drifting along in the section where the small patch stood and then returning a short time afterwards, Beth examining the cover for snakes and I glancing about for ginseng.

A tan field on the hilltop appeared. I had never seen it before. Where it came from, even in this familiar terrain, escaped me. It led nowhere.

We tried to return from the field to our starting point but couldn't. We weren't prepared for an excursion such as this and had become turned around.

As we wandered about more in search of our bearings now than ginseng, I saw the remains of an old chestnut fence cutting through the trees on the edge of the field. At points, the old rails lay atop a stone wall that I watched carefully for rattlesnakes.

Far down the crest of the Appalachians, 250 miles down that wooded ridge from the Catoctins, I found ginseng making its last stand against modern civilization. It was backed up to the crest itself, largely absent from the woodlands that bore any relationship to the low country, growing almost inside the crest, just over its lip where the ground dropped abruptly, shielded from the sweep of winds, where the crest almost burrows into itself, its earth shielded by rock outcrops.

There, the ginseng grew at the point where the earth and sky met most closely. Half of a mile into the sky, the rain fell; here, the earth enfolded headwater springs much as a giant hand cupped, covered with tulip poplar trees. The earth receives the rain first here of all places in the east, receives it best, drawing it underground where it lays beneath the covering of cohosh and ginger -- and ginseng. It receives the sun first here as well -- pure sun free of the valley haze, striking the crest without needing to work through the canopy of lower-elevation forests.

I travel there to dig ginseng and, in doing so, distinguish myself. I reach the crest here. I climb the last of the slopes, and the steepest.

I find grouse in the moist draws where the land begins to slant and hold the rain. There in the coolness and in the ground plants that grouse feed on, I found a family of them yesterday, nearly grown, and found a small patch of ginseng nearby. One of the finest ways for a grouse hunter to locate birds is to locate ginseng, because the two both like to live among the black cohosh and wild ginger growing up against the crest.

We re-entered the dense forest, and there beside large black cohosh plants were large ginseng plants, one of them with a thick stem and four branches rather than the typical three. The root would no doubt be large and heavy. Even amidst the concerns of being lost, I appreciated seeing the rare plant and considered the walk a success.

I declined to harvest those plants because of regulations within Catoctin Mountain Park and Cunningham Falls State Park. I felt no need to do so, since the hunt for the plant provides greater satisfaction than the possession of the root itself.

I knew why the plant grew on this mountain. At close to 2000 feet, the elevation cooled the climate and created conditions similar to those to the north, in Pennsylvania, where I had often hunted ginseng. There, along trout streams amid the sugar maple and tulip poplar, I had found the cool atmosphere that the plant requires, together with the rich soil created by decades of leaf decay.

Ginseng hunting removes me from the world -- which is why I consider it a high-quality form of recreation. Yet, nowhere is recreation defined more sharply than it is in this activity. There must be a point where it ends, where recreation is complete, because we are no longer ginseng hunters in America. There are now too many people and too few ginseng plants.

Autumn, mid-September, is the harvest period for ginseng roots. In the hills of western Pennsylvania, I knew it as a time of gentle rain and silence. I think back to a late afternoon when the rain had just begun to fall in the colored woods, not yet enough to penetrate the roof of leaves.

My father and I drifted over the top of a ridge from where deep hollows dropped off toward a rushing creek. There, far back in the silence, ginseng plants grew. We stooped to dig in the fine, rich ground at each sighting of golden leaves. The soil was rich enough that beech trees grew there, and the air cool enough that hemlocks stood beneath the hardwoods.

On the Blue Ridge one September day, I walked along past a witchhazel in yellow bloom, following a path leading over ground once occupied but now silent. I stopped along the trail in the coolness and pried an early settler's medicine bottle from the earth.

With the sour gums turning color in August, autumn comes early to end the year's life on the ridgetops. Yet, the Blue Ridge offered me a plant that day that made me look back fondly over the many seasons that had passed over these woods, providing a sense of continuity rather than ending. Along a fire lane, ginseng plants, golden-yellow, stood.

The day I found that ginseng on the Blue Ridge was the first day I had visited those mountains. I seek it out on every mountaintop now, as on the crest of the Catoctins. It provides a glimpse of a time when nature gave us all we needed. To see a ginseng plant is to free oneself of the complex struggle of this age. Like the tops of ridges, these glimpses endure.

Foxville Ridge features a campground at its highest point. The sites are well-maintained, the fee reasonable. I recommend this ridge at the height of summer, when it offers a strong contrast with the heat and humidity of the valley below along Route 15. The trail proves rocky, making leather boots preferable. A rattlesnake den lies near the adjacent Catoctin Trail, reinforcing this recommendation.

Ginseng grows throughout the woods surrounding this route. As elsewhere within its range, it grows sparingly there. However, the general understanding in the park that hikers leave plants undisturbed makes this forest a setting sanctioned for learning about ginseng and other native plants.

The illustration is from the Catoctin Furnace, Maryland 7.5-minute topographic quadrangle.

PORCUPINES

On Route 66, the village of Marienville stands on the edge of northwestern Pennsylvania's Allegheny National Forest. The northernmost road running to the right becomes dirt at the outskirts of town and runs to an intersection, where a left turn leads in several miles to the hamlet of Duhring. A bridge crosses Spring Creek here and a road follows the creek downstream. The ridge lies on the left, overlooking a collection of hunting camps known as Parrish.

This ridge introduces wildness to the landscape by bringing with it a particular animal. It is something of a symbol of uncivilized country, a part of our lore and language but an animal generally seen only by those who spend much time outside -- the porcupine.

I saw one roadkilled on the ridge south of State College, where the rock crest crowds the side of the pavement, and the proximity of such an uncivilized creature to such a civilized place surprised me. I know porcupines from the remote places; and, while I can't say I have never seen a porcupine in a valley, they almost invariably live on the highest sites.

That's because porcupines are not complicated. They are crude animals that dwell around rock crevices and cliffs. Like some creature that never developed advanced life skills, they carry on a simple existence, climbing their trees, eating bark, climbing down and scaling another trunk.

They are unable to move with any quickness. They possess no beauty. They possess quills, instead.

Onward they amble -- over the plateau, with ridge upon ridge of the maple-filled Allegheny National Forest beyond; in a crevice amidst the laurel far above the First Fork of the Sinnemahoning, where the simple verticality of the climb is a trek into backcountry.

In the Allegheny National Forest, porcupines appreciate the maple-cherry forests in areas such as the Spring Creek watershed to the extent that they help to support the reintroduction of the fisher, an animal hunted and trapped to extinction in that area during the nineteenth century.

Porcupines live on the ridges because their favorite foods grow there. They love the bark of birch, eating it from the trunks of successive trees. Rather than groundhog dens, as in the valleys, the ridges feature porcupine dens. The deposits of droppings betray the sites as much as anything else: rabbit-like, but situated in rock crevices where no rabbits live.

The porcupine (*Erethizon dorsatum*), also known as the hedgehog, measures around 3 feet in length as an adult, attaining a weight of over 20 pounds. Adults bear a single young. Porcupines live to an age of perhaps 10 years.

In appearance, the animal is chiefly blackish, with whitish hairs mingled in over the sides and upperparts. The face resembles a pig's snout, decidedly unappealing.

While going about its bark-eating activities, a porcupine is often very limited in its movements, spending weeks in a small stand of trees. The animal craves salt, and it often finds it in the traces of human sweat evident on the wood of log cabins in the forest. The wood of these cabins is consumed as if it were a tree.

The quills of the porcupine are white, tipped with black and furnished with barbs at the end which slant backwards and work into the skin of any creature victimized by them. The animal extends the quills outward; they remain attached during the process rather than shooting through the air, as some maintain.

When approached, porcupines turn their back to their enemies, at the same time hiding their head as much as possible. Their tail waves back and forth. Throw a shirt or blanket on the animal's back and quills will stick everywhere in it.

The sounds porcupines occasionally make bely their undistinguished appearance. They include a shriek sometimes mistaken for that of a mountain lion, moans, squeaks, and barks.

On some quiet and isolated ridgetop, a person stands an excellent chance of seeing a porcupine because nothing in particular threatens their existence. Despite their vulnerability to human attack, no-one considers them of enough value to hunt them out.

Perhaps the most memorable impression they convey is that of their unhurried movements -- as if the pace of the world had indeed been left behind in the quiet of the high places they colonize.

I prefer to hike the Allegheny National Forest after mid-May, because prior to that, the Canadian-like climate produces forbidding clouds and chill. August provides the most consistent weather. The walk to Spring Creek Ridge leads into rocky country, rattlesnake country, so I advise high leather boots.

The illustration is from the Hallton, Pennsylvania 7.5-minute topographic quadrangle.

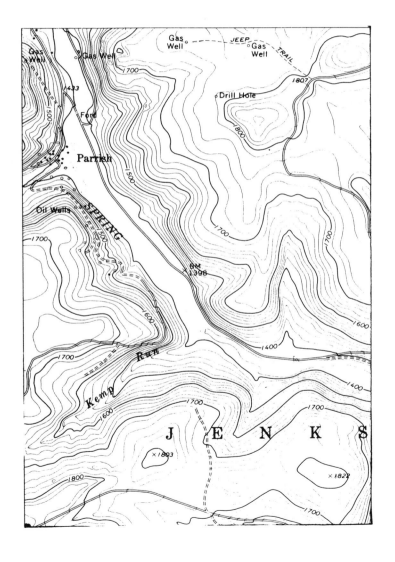

HEARTS CONTENT

To reach Hearts Content Ridge, drive over Route 6 across the northern tier of Pennsylvania to the town of Sheffield, at the edge of the Allegheny National Forest. A road cuts across the forest from near Sheffield to the hamlet of Dunham Siding, the nearest location to Hearts Content.

The hike here leads through a stand of virgin conifer timber over a well-established path. Nearby runs the North Country Trail, which offers opportunities for extended backpacking trips. The hike at Hearts Content begins at a National Forest Recreation Area.

Up on ridges such as Hearts Content Ridge, away from the cultivated and altered land, "weeds" do not occur. Weeds represent a response to regular and severe abuse of the earth, something which ridges see less of -- and, in a few instances, have never seen any of.

Man never altered Hearts Content Natural Area, on the ridge above Pennsylvania's Allegheny River, where a virgin forest of white pine stands. He never altered the crest of many mountains in the southern highlands where rhododendron growth offered nothing to log; nor rock formations on various ridges -- unchanged places.

The most significant alternative to weeds in the east is hayscented fern (*Dennstaedtia punctilobula*). It mends the disturbances of man in places of infrequent contact such as that caused by the logging at the turn of the century. Though I see it on most ridges I hike, in certain instances, it hints of untouched ground, such as that of ridges subjected to climatic extremes and never timbered, where it springs up in the fresh light admitted with the dying off of trees.

Seeing hayscented fern at Hearts Content, I realize that it has always sprung up in beds there, visible to the Indians in the same way as to myself. When a pine falls and light strikes the earth, it appears. It is a scarce element of green amidst the brown of pine needles and tree trunks.

In the Black Mountains of North Carolina, red spruce trees stand, virgin, like the white pines of Hearts Content. In the coolness, a tree falls, leaving an opening. Hayscented ferns appear.

The abundance of this fern carries it as close to the concept of weed as wild country allows. Miles upon miles of the high plateau at the headwaters of the Allegheny River are green with hayscented fern. Whereas other species occur in isolated patches or small beds, as wildflowers might, this fern spreads like a fragrant grass.

When the sun shines on this plant, it brings out a bright sweetness. Humidity, even without the presence of sunlight, brings out a similar scent, while the physical decline of the plants in autumn produces a fragrance with different qualities.

For today, hayscented fern produces the finest "meadow" that the modern day wilderness affords. Wherever the land lies unbroken by a plow, its seed lies ready to spring forth as a response to a falling treetrunk. It is an element lying in the makeup of untouched places.

The hike here runs over a piece of flat ground with soft footing. The North Country Trail recommends itself with similar settings. I suggest August for a hike here, when summer has settled in fully into this northernmost portion of the mid-Atlantic region.

The illustration is from the Cherry Grove, Pennsylvania 7.5-minute topographic quadrangle.

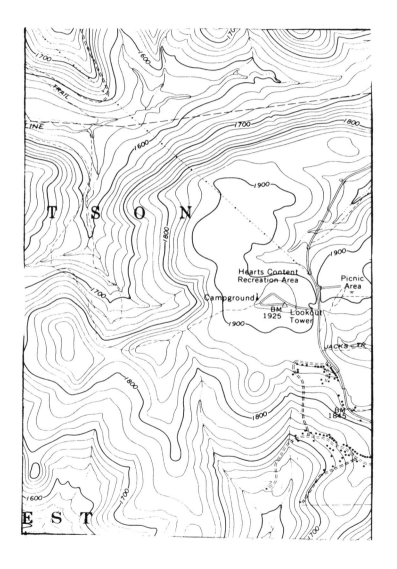

BLACK FOREST

To reach Black Forest Ridge, drive over Route 6 west through Pennsylvania's northern counties. At the town of Galeton, turn south on Route 144 and follow it to the hamlet of Oleona, where it merges with Route 44. Follow 44 toward Watertown.

Route 44 continues toward the town of Jersey Shore, on the West Branch of the Susquehanna River. Where the road passes through Lycoming County's Tiadaghton State Forest, a road known as Narrow Gage Road branches off to the left. A short distance down Route 44, another road enters from the left. Follow this to a gate where the Highwood Trail begins. This trail passes through a stand of virgin red pine, a tree seldom viewed in the Mid-Atlantic.

Natives of Pennsylvania use the term "Black Forest" loosely to identify a vast stretch of their north woods country, but only a certain locale in those woods bears the name "Black Forest" on signs, storefronts -- Black Forest Inn, Black Forest Trail. Yet, around that locale stand treetrunks indistinguishable from those standing fifty miles in all directions. What separates this collection of trees from those that surround them, conjuring up the name?

Certain qualities of environment produce this recognition. Grasping these qualities demands the effort of pausing and waiting, but within those qualities resides the very source of the Black Forest ; within that source, the Black Forest's entirety.

The quality of silence constitutes the entry point for this recognition. It manifests itself as an excessive silence, a dramatic backdrop. The person who leaves the car and stands along Route 44, behind the cushioning presence of miles of densely-spaced treetrunks -- growing more closely than in other areas -- finds this entry point immediately.

At some juncture not far along from this beginning of awareness come rain and fog -- excessive rain and fog more a part of the ridgetop than a part of the weather, rain and fog extending beyond our ideas of limits or extremes.

Crossing this foggy and silent border of extremes, evergreen boughs appear, silent evergreen boughs from trees little-known in Pennsylvania. On this ridge, the hemlock shadows are, in fact, spruce shadows. The white pines are red pines. Larches stand about, seeded of their own accord rather than planted by mine reclamation personnel. The person standing among these trees realizes that the Black Forest stands around him.

The white birches of the northern latitudes stand on the ridge in numbers, without limitations of ecology, undiminished by the bark-gatherers who exploit the birches growing in sparse patterns of low-lying country. The mystique of white birch firewood lives here. The logs crackle and flame even when wet, the flammable bark guarding wood that burns without spark or smoke.

The white birch is perhaps the most distinctive tree in America. A northern species occurring from Newfoundland across to Alaska, and from New England west through the northern states, it becomes a tree of ridgetops from Pennsylvania southward. Though other species are pale in hue, absolute whiteness covers the trunks of white birches, a color rather scarce in nature.

The snow-white bark is accented with black scars at the bases of the branches; horizontal dashes encircle it. It finds more than a merely whimsical use as paper: a pen writes as clearly on its surface as on that of any store-bought product.

White birch bark peels from the trees in large sheets, and Indians used this bark to sheathe their canoes by binding it to the frames of the boats. Today, we use it widely in any craft work demanding a rustic appearance.

This tree normally attains a height of 40 or 50 feet. It produces wood in sufficient quantity to furnish flooring and trim, as well as minor objects such as spools. The leaves are modest, small in size and shaped somewhat like those of a cherry tree.

Red pine, like white birch, becomes a ridgetop tree in the southern part of its range. No other tree in the forest displays an orangish trunk. The heartwood of red pine carries out this reddish pattern.

This pine grows from Nova Scotia and Newfoundland west to Manitoba and Minnesota. It occurs southward through New England into Pennsylvania, Michigan and Wisconsin.

Foresters make efforts to introduce red pine on various sites. The resulting stands of straight, tall trees produce valuable lumber. All red pines, small or large, bear long needles, the longest of any conifer in the northeast, which contribute to a classical appearance. The long needles fill out the form of the red pine and make it a splendid Christmas tree, notable for its durability.

Like the white birch (*Betula papyrifera*) and red pine (*Pinus resinosa*), the larch, or tamarack (*Larix laricina*) is a north country tree, occurring from the Yukon east to the Canadian Atlantic coast, southward to Alaska and, in the east, New England, Pennsylvania, and the Great Lakes region. Not large trees, they average perhaps 50 feet in height. The needles of the tree are like short brushes. They fall in autumn. Many people know the tamarack as an unglamorous tree planted on the waste heaps of coal mines to prevent erosion, or as the tree whose straight trunks become telephone poles.

The elevation of this ridgetop creates a strip of north country befitting the German name "Black Forest". The larch and pine and spruce are extended southward by an entire ridge of north country rather than an isolated occurrence. The German settlers found this country similar to that in Germany's Black Forest.

Within this ridgetop consciousness dwells not only the source of a name but of part of America's outdoor sports tradition transplanted from the Old World. Deer hunting reaches a high point on this ridge: 40 and more deer sighted on a typical evening. Every stream that surfaces from the mist and rain of this ridge holds trout to flyfish for. Just as the source of the silent letters "Black Forest" is mute and invisible, so is the heart of this living tradition of the wilderness. Yet, we know that it lives within these particular trees, this ridge.

This trail represents one of many in an area crossed by a number of ski trails as well as designated footpaths. To derive the most pleasure from them, visit after the cold spells of late spring recede, generally by mid-June.

The illustration is from the Slate Run, Pennsylvania 7.5-minute topographic quadrangle.

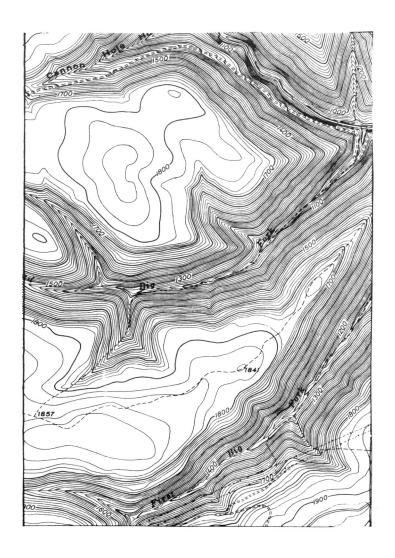

WILDFLOWERS

Big Pine Flat Ridge lies in the heart of south-central Pennsylvania's Michaux State Forest. Traveling Route 81, Exit 6 at Chambersburg leads east on Route 30 to Caledonia State Park. Route 233 runs north into the woods. The first through-road to the left, a dirt road, leads past Long Pine Run Reservoir. Continuing straight ahead past a road cut covered with rhododendrons, two side roads enter from the right in quick succession. Continuing uphill, an intersection appears with ample parking space and signs indicating the Appalachian Trail.

Big Pine Flat Ridge shows how, despite the fact that ridges take on names of mountain ranges as they run southward, and pass through states, their true changes involve the living things appearing on them. Simple and eloquent species succeed each other on the ridgetops.

A wildflower called starflower (*Trientalis borealis*) symbolizes the nature of the flowers that appear on the crests. It suggests, as well, the pattern of the cool north country that follows the high places southward.

Starflower proves singular in its evocative geometry, its blossom comprised of six or seven star-white rays running outward like those of a paper-cut star. Balancing the pattern, five-to-nine leaves radiate outward -- larger star rays.

One June day beside a high country marsh at the northern end of the mid-Atlantic region, Pennsylvania's Tamarack Swamp, the white starflower blossoms reminded me of snow. The ridgetop climate stung my hands with cold, especially as I went about gathering tamarack cones for craftwork.

Again I came upon starflower, 100 miles south amidst a gypsy-moth-ridden oak forest. There, where ridgetop hayscented fern had responded to the fresh burst of sunlight from the leafless woods, a bed of the flowers stood as well. Their foliage had a fresh greenness representative of the breeziness and quiet of the place.

Once again I saw it, this time amidst a forest virtually devoid of wildflowers, barren ground for the most part beneath the shadows of the leaves and straight treetrunks. However, a brief opening appeared near where the sun struck the top of the sparsely forested ridge. There a miniature display of wildflowers brightened the ground: fringed polygala (*Polygala paucifolia*), and starflower, as if white stars had fallen from the sky and found the high ground first. The place is a well-known one: the Susquehannock Trail overlooking Pennsylvania's Ole Bull State Park.

The flowers of the ridgetops remain little-known even to those involved with the subject. Most regard them as rare wildflowers, perhaps because they represent a class of distinctive and decorative species. In reality, they present themselves to anyone frequenting the high places.

I recall an encounter with a wildflower known as pipsissewa (*Chimaphila umbellata*) on the top of Mount Nittany, overlooking Penn State University. I identified it through its dark, glossy leaves and pink flowers, which carried a sweet fragrance. On Nittany, it grew among mountain laurel and blueberry; I found it above the Ohio River on a knoll covered with a cushion of moss. Pipsissewa occurs southward to Georgia in the mountain environment.

Early in my hiking days, a patch of pink ladyslipper orchids startled me. They stood on the very crest of the ridge above the Allegheny River, amidst American chestnut saplings attempting to withstand the chestnut blight.

Pink ladyslippers (*Cypripedium acaule*) are one of the most spectacular wildflowers in the eastern United States. They consist of a blossom up to two inches long, pink in color, positioned on a straight stem rising from a pair of leaves at ground level. Expect these flowers on mossy ground on ridgetops. They occur south to Georgia in the mountains. Like starflower, pipsissewa, fringed polygala, trailing arbutus and wild azalea, they thrive in the coolness north to Canada.

Yesterday, on Big Pine Flat Ridge, I took a walk along a high section of the Appalachian Trail and renewed my acquaintance with perhaps the most famous of the ridgetop flowers. Walking along, I noticed that, in the cleared strip of the trail itself, moss covered the ground. Moss typically accompanies trailing arbutus, an early spring blossom known for its fragrance. I soon noted arbutus plants there as I walked along, the final lace of icy snow fading away atop the oak leaves.

The fragrance of the tiny and star-like trailing arbutus is perhaps the strongest scent in the entire forest. A few sprigs of the plant, its leaves miniature ovals, rough-textured and evergreen, retain their scent for an entire week, a fragrance sweet and refined, deservant of a commercial identification.

Trailing arbutus illustrates how misconceptions grow up regarding the abundance or scarcity of a particular plant or animal. In regions where its habitat is reduced greatly, trailing arbutus is reduced greatly. However, this plant, within the hundreds of miles of ridgetop habitat, is not in itself a rare plant. I expect to see it on the crests rather than simply hope to see it.

Outdoorsmen should make a point of locating trailing arbutus for the sake of the fragrance. Fortunately, the trails and dirt roads of the crests enhance its habitat, since it appreciates sloped ground on the edges of openings. Learning to recognize its leaves in other seasons promises a look at the blossoms in spring.

Trailing arbutus (*Epigaea repens*) occurs with unusual regularity in south-central Pennsylvania. This is a function of poor soil. The oak woods it prefers colonize rocky and weak ground that fails to grow even trees of respectable size.

As I approached the crest of a knoll above the Ohio River, I detected a sweet fragrance. I looked about and, in time, found a shrub brightening the woods with pink, each blossom resembling that of a honeysuckle -- wild azalea.

I look for wild azaleas on the ridges every spring, late in the season when the sun shines brightly and strongly through the trees, yet no leaves shade the ground, owing to the habit of the oak trees there to leaf out after other species. The fragrance of the blossoms is the most noticeable in the entire ridgetop environment. It drifts through the air for yards.

Flowers such as these extend spring into June on the ridge. With the sour gums turning red by August, these places may see as little as two months of true summer, even at the latitude of the mid-Atlantic states. Yet, the fragrance and brightness of such plants compensate for that shortfall and make the ridge, rather than something less, a full environment unto itself.

I recommend this hike in May, when the azaleas and ladyslippers bloom. October, an otherwise favored period for hiking, offers less in this area than in others due to a lack of softwood trees providing autumn colors. Fall color here appears in hardwood foliage that peaks around the beginning of November, frequently amidst unpleasant weather.

The illustration is from the Caledonia Park, Pennsylvania 7.5-minute topographic quadrangle.

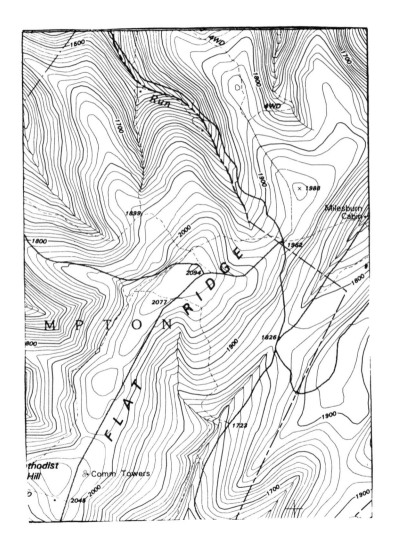

CHESTNUT

Nittany Ridge commands the skyline above Penn State University. Reaching the top of it on foot represents something of a custom for students at the university; hence, a footpath ascending the mountain. On Route 26, only a mile or so from the university grounds, an exit leads to the village of Lemont. In view of the main street is an old Greek Orthodox church. The side road bypassing it climbs out of town, bends left and ends at a small parking lot facing the trail.

Once atop the ridge, the path follows the crest along rock outcrops. Where it initially breaks out onto the ridge, it offers a scenic view. The hike follows the ridge for about 1 mile before reaching private property.

A tree from the past grows on Mount Nittany. I knew it years ago from a hike I took that passed by a property boundary. A fencepost standing before me was fashioned from an extraordinary type of wood. It had outlasted everything -- property owners, the barbed wire attached with staples -- until it stood in the midst of a forest that had risen up in the intervening years.

I had long assumed that the post was fashioned from the customary black locust. However, the trees surrounding it were beech and sugar maple, among which a locust would rarely grow.

What was this wood that radically outlasted all native woods? If after 25 years a typical fencepost rots and breaks off at ground level, why was this one still sound after almost 100?

Curious, I split a piece of it. I found warm-colored wood with a fresh appearance, the grain straight and uninterrupted, the surface free of the splinters that the yellow colored locust is known for -- American chestnut; it could be nothing else.

This chestnut post was a ghost of the early American forest. Chestnut (*Castanea dentata*) was the dominant tree of the Appalachian mountains until the early twentieth century, when it was attacked by a blight that virtually destroyed the species, leaving current generations to grow up without chestnuts covering the ground in autumn.

Chestnut blight first came to our notice in America in 1904, having originated in the Orient. It spread throughout the range of the American chestnut and reached the southern portion of it by the 1920's. The original range of the tree encompassed the region from southern Maine to Mississippi, westward to Michigan and Illinois.

Unlike walnuts or butternuts, which are housed in hard shells, chestnuts come within a prickly case of sorts known as a burr. These burrs are visible throughout the winter as they lie on the ground, large as apples.

Today, considerable effort centers around reviving the American chestnut tree. No botanical scheme yet has succeeded, because the spores of chestnut blight remain in the dead chestnut wood lying about. Through extensive investigation, researchers have located occasional trees which attain full size and remain resistant to blight; they focus their studies on these.

American chestnut played a large role in the outdoor history of the East. One hundred years ago, when trappers pursued black bears for their hides, the custom was to set traps along ridges forested with chestnut trees. In the fall, bears were attracted in numbers to the fallen chestnuts. Likewise, wild turkeys thrived in great flocks during the chestnut era, part of an entire array of wildlife that a widespread tree such as this could support.

I examined similar fenceposts in my woods and found them to be, as much as fenceposts, archaeological statements. Where the wire had been fastened to them, they were riddled with ancient staples, and nails protruded from the surface -- not the nails we use today, but square-headed ones, nineteenth-century nails. The wood had a seasoned appearance, a silvery cast brought on by exposure to the sun and rain. Some of it bore maroon and brown streaks.

I gathered enough of those posts to lay them in a zig-zag fence like those seen in the Blue Ridge mountains. One day, I cut a piece of that fence and caught the fresh smell of a second century in it.

Some of the life's spirit of chestnut trees must live in those posts for them to stand a century. I almost anticipate their springing to life -- sprouting chestnut leaves like outsized beech leaves to glow their gold color, remaining, as is their nature, on the branches after even the leaves of the oaks have fallen. The blue backdrop of mountain crests would be theirs alone until the beginning of November, when they finally fell.

I have seen those leaves -- and I was born long after the assumed demise of the chestnut. This demise is, in reality, more of a severe decimation, because stunted chestnut trees still shoot up and survive the blight for short periods of time. Look for them on the very crests of mountains, where they associate with a class of small-sized trees like white birch and mountain ash.

The widespread destruction caused by chestnut blight, which amounted to 9 million acres of trees killed, tempts one to assign the disease to a category of insurmountable virus -- a modern plague of the botanical community. The many years intervening since the original appearance of this blight tend to reinforce such a view.

However, the knowledge to defeat the blight now exists. Researchers are engaged in the long process of implementing it.

Soon after the debilitation of our chestnut stands, researchers availed themselves of genetic cross-breeding principles in an effort to produce blight-resistant chestnuts. Around 1920, the United States Department of Agriculture initiated an earnest effort aimed at defeating the blight by crossing Chinese Chestnut and American Chestnut trees.

CHESTNUT

Researchers assumed, rightly so, that Chinese Chestnut trees possessed immunity from the blight, since the disease originated in the Orient. They crossed Chinese and American Chestnuts and then proceeded to cross the resulting hybrids back to Chinese Chestnut trees in an effort to build up the immunity in the test trees.

The initiative failed. In 1960, we abandoned it.

In the late 1970s, Charles R. Burnham, a Minnesota geneticist, encountered the knowledge leading to what experts see as the imminent salvation of the American Chestnut tree. He crossed Chinese and American Chestnuts, but then, rather than crossing back to Chinese Chestnuts, he crossed back to American Chestnuts.

Bruce Wood, horticulturist with the U.S.D.A., explained that the initial cross in the scheme, that between Chinese and American Chestnuts, produces a hybrid with qualities of blight resistance. That hybrid, referred to as the F-1 generation, still contains some residue of Chinese Chestnut, so we cross it back with an American Chestnut, reducing the presence of Chinese Chestnut in the tree yet continuing to enhance blight resistance through the presence of the Chinese Chestnut element.

Ann Leffel, of the Pennsylvania chapter of the American Chestnut Foundation, an organization established in 1983 with President Jimmy Carter as an honorary director, explained that the scheme involves 3 back-crosses to American Chestnuts, followed

84

by an intercross among the blight-resistant trees produced. By the sixth generation of trees, only the tree remains which represents the beginning of the restoration of our chestnut. One-sixteenth of the trees produced during such an intercross possess a full set of resistant genes segregated according to a genetic code. The final product is 95-percent American, 5-percent Chinese, chestnut.

We await this tree. Yan Shi, research scientist at the American Chestnut Foundation's headquarters in Meadowview, Virginia, estimates a date of around 2005. The furthest progression of genetic crossing now involves small numbers of trees in a third back-crossing.

Jerry Payne, who worked with the U.S.D.A. on American Chestnuts, pointed out that Chinese Chestnuts offer no potential for reforestation because they grow in a spreading pattern where they take advantage of field and orchard habitats. Released in a forest environment, they succumb to competition from species of trees that grow straight upward, eventually blocking the sun. Hence, the current effort to cross to American Chestnuts.

At this point, Bruce Wood estimates we stand 30-40 years from the development of a genetically engineered chestnut. This alternative holds promise, but the results of back-crossing are more immediate.

Recently, the Chestnut Foundation cooperated with the federal government in planting nuts from chestnut trees produced within the first back-cross of the genetic scheme. The planting took place in the Allegheny National Forest of northwestern Pennsylvania, around a clear-cut area.

Ann Leffel explained that one-fourth of the trees that grow from this planting should live for 25 years, the remainder vanishing. The need of the new trees for the open light around logged areas complements the potential to provide wildlife food in such areas.

In Meadowview, Virginia, where around 5000 trees grow in the research area of the Chestnut Foundation, the American Chestnut stands poised for its revival. Already, we look forward to working with nature in finding the most effective means of spreading the thousands and thousands of chestnut trees necessary for this effort into the forest environment. With the current assault on the mountaintop environment from acid rain and insects, our emerging abilities gain immediacy.

The nuts of the chestnut appear now and then on trees that manage vigorous growth, both the prickly burrs enclosing them and the nuts themselves chestnut-brown in color. When I do find them, it is on the edges of woods roads or logging cuts, where the fresh burst of light provides encouraging conditions for growth.

Other chestnut artifacts survive in the latter-day woods. There are, of course, stumps and logs, but since their silvery-gray is similar to the color assumed by other old stumps and logs, all but the unusually perceptive hiker bypasses them. To discover old chestnut wood, look for a gray-colored stump or snag with a hollow heart and a sweet birch tree sprouting from its center. Sweet, or black, birch has a notable affinity for the acidic mulch produced by rotting chestnut.

This past autumn, I walked over a rock-covered Appalachian ridge, munching on blueberries, when I chanced upon a deposit of wood knots arrayed beside a rotting log. They had lain there for so long that green lichens had taken up residence on their surfaces, perhaps taking them for rocks. Sliced with a saw, the wood, heavy with resin, presented an agate-like surface of growth rings, rock-hard. Its solidity suggested chestnut, as did its gray tone, but a resinous fragrance proved it pine.

The rocky surfaces of the ridges keep fallen wood from contact with soil. As a result, much chestnut wood remains on the crests. Turned on a lathe and preserved with varnish, such wood has the rich brown color of November oak ridges and can become, among other things, a stylish reel seat for a hand-crafted flyrod. Increasingly, chestnut fencepost fragments are converted into small items such as vases and sold at crafts fairs.

Such items preserve the brown color peculiar to chestnut. They enable us to understand why hair is labeled "chestnut-brown" or a horse described as a "chestnut mare."

The chestnut spirit has an ultimate use, one that may do more than any other to ensure its role in our cultural consciousness. This is one of the finest firewoods known, white birch included.

Because it is not generally available, the popular tables ranking the firewoods have neglected it.

When lit, a pale yellow flame licks outward in an unhurried fashion, free of visible smoke or uneven motion, as if from a thick candle. The wood is eventually consumed, but not before a long interlude spent staring at the flames has passed.

The first chestnut wood I ever burnt came from a fencepost standing in my hills, and in it was a legacy, a post freshly split settling into the ground sometime in the 1800s. Anyone traveling by it on the day it was driven into the ground did so in a horse-drawn buggy. The graceful and easy days passed by, as it acquired the gray cast of a December sky and the status of a natural monument.

In the case of Nittany Ridge, a summer hike means less company from students hiking at the beginning of fall semester and close of winter semester in April, but autumn presents an opportunity to view the chestnut leaves in their gold color, which makes them easy to identify. The chestnuts here stand close to the trail, not obscured by brush, as in many other locations where they grow.

The illustration is from the State College, Pennsylvania 7.5-minute topographic quadrangle.

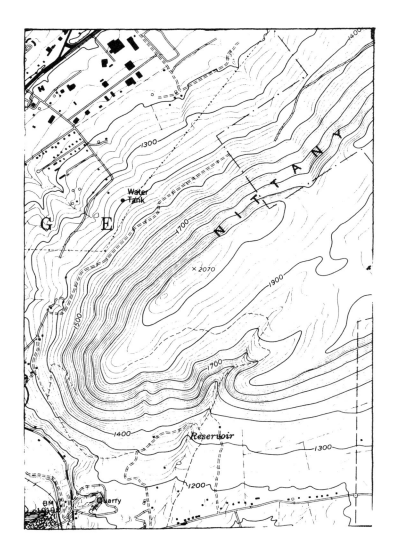

WINTERGREEN

Tussey Ridge runs for a long distance near State College, Pennsylvania, and Penn State University, but at one point, it offers a defining walk along its crest. About 7 miles south of State College, near the village of Pine Grove Mills, Route 26 climbs to a popular lookout with a generous parking area. A trail bisects Route 26 at this point, emerging at a woods road directly across the highway and carrying on into the woods at the southern end of the parking lot. Called the Jackson Trail, this stretch provides a hike of at least 6 miles. It makes up part of the large Mid-State Trail system.

On the Appalachian ridgetops of central Pennsylvania, lines of wilderness run southward, marked by the trunks of white birches growing from rock heaps and, overhead, ravens croaking. I walked Tussey Ridge on a February day, around me in the silence growing the few plants willing to resist the environment of wind and cold.

Ahead, where tree growth was regenerating itself beneath a grove of oaks killed by gypsy moths, amber color, the amber of sweet birch branches, attracted my eye to a thicket of the trees. I realized that I had made contact with an element of nature that mountain people had interacted with for generations, one of the mountain teas.

The sweet birch occurs in a variety of habitats, but it is an essential element of mountaintop flora, a counterpart to the weedy wild cherry of populated areas; since hundreds grew in this thicket, I felt free to pull two saplings up by the roots. Fresh from the ground, they showed a red color and featured the fragrance of wintergreen that distinguished this tree of ordinary features from the others of these woods. I packed the roots off of the ridge with me, planning to shave off the bark, dry it and store it in a bag.

I walked a few hundred yards along the crest and stepped among patches of late snow to the edge of a clearing. Here and there grew wintergreen plants with shiny leaves that carried a teaberry fragrance like that of the sweet birches. I was some distance from the prime wintergreen patches in these mountains, patches that covered the ground with big leaves and red berries that drooped from the inch-high plants throughout the winter, but I nevertheless gathered a handful of leaves that included a number that were large and purple-colored. Low elevations comprise no botanical barrier to wintergreen (*Gaultheria procumbens*), but the general distribution of plants on the mountain ridges defines it as a mountain plant.

The winter grayness opened above me as I carried my birch and wintergreen onto the cleared corridor of a woods road, along which grew a humble shrub with brown leaves clinging to its branches. I began crushing those leaves, my hands taking on a sharp fragrance as I worked. The leaves bore a fragrance in the summer, but the months of cold had sweetened them further and produced a fine tobacco of sorts that I added to my collection of tea materials. The plant was sweetfern (*Comptonia peregrina*), a species unknown on streets and in cultivated valleys.

All three of the teas now in my pack were classic beverages of the mountains -- not edible curiosities consumed to prove a point. All of them were recognizable throughout the year and all preferred mountain habitat. It was the sweetfern that intrigued me the most, because it had potential as a wild drink of high caliber but had received little attention in outdoor publications.

Though the ranges of these plants extend beyond central Pennsylvania, the mountains there offer optimum habitat. Plants do not occur evenly within maps of their ranges; rather, they appear rarely within portions of such areas and abundantly in other localities. The stony and thin soil in central Pennsylvania provides ideal conditions for sweet birch, sweetfern and wintergreen.

At home, I tossed the fragmented sweetfern leaves into a pan and covered them with water, finding that the ingredients in the dried material resulted in a brown-colored drink as the water heated. The fragrance remained in the pleasant taste of the beverage, the leaf bits clinging to the bottom of the pan and allowing me to pour a clean sample. This essence of sweetfern survived after the addition of sugar. Since the dried bits of leaf had the appearance of supermarket tea, I realized that they could be packed into teabags and steeped as a reasonable substitute. The notable simplicity of sweetfern harvesting, an activity free of heat and summer insects -- and the fine flavor of the tea -- would make the effort a worthwhile one.

Sweetfern leaves, of course, also provide tea in the fresh state, at the same time offering the chance to identify the plant. Its leaves, fern-like on the edges, grow from wiry twigs that spring from a plant suggestive of a shrub in its pattern of growth. It is a species of cleared soil and restricts itself to that habitat, remaining an unknown object to those who confine their hikes to deep woods.

Unlike the sweetfern I had gathered, the wintergreen in my pack would lose its scent and usefulness upon drying, a process that began when I emerged from the laurel and descended the road to the village in the valley. Since I wanted a drink that was pleasant and not merely non-poisonous, I knew that I had to use my wintergreen at the earliest convenience.

Prior experience had impressed upon me the strength of wintergreen tea, the orange beverage resulting from a handful of the teaberry-scented leaves steeped in hot water. However, an uninspiring flavor proved that the fragrance of the leaves dissipated as the tea boiled, in a manner similar to that involved with the drying process.

I later learned to conserve the wintergreen fragrance by packing a jar tightly with fresh leaves and filling it with boiling water. As the jar stood in an undisturbed state for two days, bubbles and a fizzing sound told of the spreading of the fragrant oils. When the jar was covered and heated and the tea then poured, the essence of wintergreen filled the beverage.

The root bark of the sweet birch contains more potency than leaves of wintergreen, so the recipe for birch tea involves only a teaspoon of the shavings in a cup of boiling water, steeped for five minutes away from the heat. A handful of sweet birch root bark carries more than a teaberry fragrance. Its full sweetness makes it smell like a piece of wintergreen candy.

The tea that the bark yields is peach-colored and clear, carrying the flavor of wintergreen well without the special treatment that wintergreen leaves demand and, of course, without the caffeine contained in traditional tea. Then, too, a heap of the shavings lends itself well to drying and storage in teabags, which saves forays into the woods at times when the soil around the roots is frozen.

Should freezing weather make obtaining the roots impractical, the shavings of twigs offer a substitute. Browsing deer find essential ingredients in these limbs and provide diversion for the forager as they flee through the thickets of sweet birch that spring up in the wake of logging cuts.

Walking through the birch thickets during the season of winter teas has a domestic kind of appeal never more evident than during the midseason thaws. Then, the wind relaxes on the mountainsides, which fill up with mist and rain. The sweet fern becomes sodden, the wintergreen leaves fresh, the reddish trunks of the sweet birches lacquered with wetness and a suggestion of coming spring.

This trail on Tussey Ridge represents the rockiest path I have ever hiked. For that reason, I advise leather boots. I recommend the path in summer or early autumn, when the breeze on this ridge dispels insects and the elevation maintains the temperature at a refreshing level. Chilly weather lingers here into May, while winter in this part of the mid-Atlantic generally proves severe.

The illustration is from the Pine Grove Mills, Pennsylvania 7.5-minute topographic quadrangle.

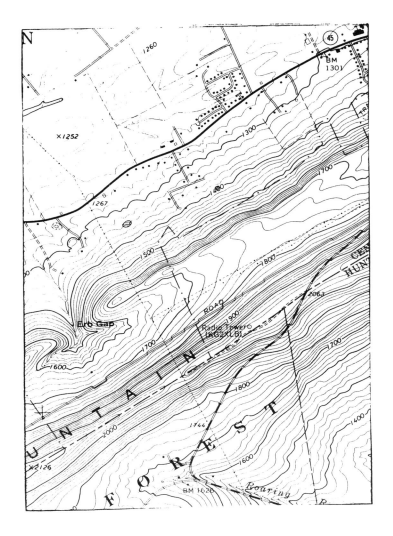

BLACK CHERRY

Cherry Ridge lies behind Ole Bull State Park, reached by way of Route 6 to the town of Galeton, Pennsylvania, then Route 144 south. A well-known trail, the Susquehannock Trail, bisects the state park and climbs northwest up a small stream onto the ridgetop. The park offers a large amount of parking space for both day-hikers and backpackers.

Cherry Ridge serves as an unusual location where the justification for a site's name remains as that place's chief characteristic. The names the early settlers gave to locations --the Panther Rocks and Chestnut Ridges -- identify little that is real today. We shot all of the panthers a century ago, and the huge chestnut trees of the old days died of chestnut blight, giving us porcupines rather than panthers, oaks for chestnuts, leaving us with only our imaginations.

Deep in the mountains of the northern mid-Atlantic region, where a long ridge runs through the forest, there stands one of the few namesakes unchanged over the decades, as rich and abundant as in the days when its trees named a stream Cherry Run. It is a forest within a forest, a stand of black cherries that grow as trees once grew -- big and tall.

HIGH GROUND

After the lumbermen cut these woods long ago, unique conditions allowed the cherries to recreate this forest. Perhaps the stability of the environment fostered this -- a wide area of level ground -- and its richness, with a location at the head of a mountain stream.

Unlike typical cherry trees, which branch out, these continue to rise upward -- 100, 150 feet. Unlike typical treetrunks, these do not curve or bend. Lumbermen know, if the average person doesn't, the reputation of Pennsylvania black cherry wood, and here lies the source of the reputation.

I know Cherry Ridge for its silence. The silence of centuries ago, if not the wilderness namesakes, remains throughout these mountains, interrupted only on the occasion of the early lumbermens' saws and axes, and never by permanent settlement. The latter-day absence of traditional sounds -- mountain lion cries, as an example -- reinforces this silence.

Of the traditional sounds of wilderness, only one remains on Cherry Ridge: the buzz of timber rattlesnakes. I know the sound, and others who know it realize its forceful quality, the hollow and sharp rattle, carrying far amid the peace of the forest.

I remember hearing the buzz of a rattlesnake 25 years ago and sensing the totally uncivilized nature of the creature that produced it. We came upon the snake beside a popular fishing hole frequented by barefooted children; therefore, we felt the need to eliminate it.

BLACK CHERRY

My father stood in the middle of the dirt road attempting to dispatch the rattler, already run over with our car's tires, by striking it with a stick. Following the failure of that approach, and even after subsequent attacks with stones, it rose up, long and thick, striking repeatedly, rattling and rattling. I had never seen any creature maintain such a ferocious hold on life.

A rattlesnake hunter told me of a den on Cherry Ridge. As to the intimate details of location, he retained as defensive a stance as the snakes themselves. He laid down hints on location that confused more than clarified. I produced a topographic map for him to guide me with, and his manner graded to near-hostility.

The snake-hunter's evasiveness stemmed from the fact that few rattlesnakes remain today, just as fewer and fewer mountain lions remained throughout the nineteenth century. Their dens lie far up the mountains, amid the stone and laurel of the ridgetops where the sun awakens them each spring from hibernation and warms them, where the blue of far-off ridges is brushed behind the tops of trees.

A thick-bodied snake up to five feet in length, with a triangular head and pattern of triangles on its back cut sharp and clean, as if from stone, the timber rattler (*Crotalus horridus*) ranges throughout the mountainous country of the east. The color pattern of a black-phase timber rattler, with elements of black, tan and gray, suggests that of a ruffed grouse's feathers. Though nearly extinct in that part of its range lying in New England, it still occurs in fair quantity further south. In fact, I found three recently along the side of the road in the Catoctins of Maryland.

The fact that a rattlesnake bite results in a dangerous, even deadly, reaction leads many to attack any rattlers encountered in the forest. With the increasing scarcity of the reptile, many who once treated rattlesnakes in this manner now stress preservation and discourage such adventurism. The official status of the timber rattlesnake as a protected species supports this approach with fines for the harming of rattlers.

As early settlers oriented toward the civilizing of the new nation recoiled at the menacing defensiveness of the mountain lion, I found unpleasant the defensiveness of the man guarding his rattlesnake den. However, the episode made me realize how our current interest in the outdoors is converting it into a museum piece of sorts, with outdoor writers interpreting rattlesnakes as they might exhibits. I hope the ridgetops remain beyond our information technology, a solid basis of life, as in the early days.

I only know the den lies there on Cherry Ridge -- a good place for a rattlesnake den, in a part of the world that features some quality resistant to change.

One other sound remains on Cherry Ridge from an earlier era. It is the sound of a fife played by the ghost of a soldier slain during the French-Indian war. A book of local folklore relates the tale; one day, I confirmed it through natural means.

I heard the sound as I reached the ridge, climbing through the silence of beech woods. It consisted of a whistling, a pause, then more whistling at a different pitch. I had never heard a sound like it -- not spontaneous and unpracticed, but deliberate and accomplished. It possessed the fragile, plaintive quality of flute music. I looked around in the shadows and saw nothing.

Then I noticed the faint shape of a bird on a tree branch. The sound came again from that spot. I knew then that the fife sound was the song of a hermit thrush, a good name for a bird frequenting such a secluded place.

The hermit thrush I heard singing in the north woods of Pennsylvania that day was a nesting bird. The species breeds as far south as Virginia, but only along the mountains. Hermit thrushes nest from the Yukon through Manitoba, Quebec, Alberta, and Ontario, and in the northern states of Michigan and Minnesota eastward to Long Island.

The nest of the hermit thrush (*Hylocichla guttata faxoni*) contains 3-8 greenish-blue eggs. Built of moss, twigs, leaves and other minor objects, it frequently sits on the ground in the middle of the forest. Hermit thrushes apparently regard the depths of the woods as a refuge where they need nest only among the treetrunks rather than up on their branches.

The bird itself is only about 7 inches long. The tail and rump are brown, the head and shoulders olive, and the breast speckled white. The family of birds to which it belongs includes the robin and wood thrush.

The highly regarded song of this bird, considered by many as the finest of all bird music, consists of a series of phrases which ascend in pitch, reaching a climax and then beginning again. The sound is thin and high-pitched, devoid of the rustic quality of bird song in general.

With brown feathers to mingle with the shadows and a habit of colonizing remote forests, the hermit thrush lends itself to a ghost identity. At the time the events of the ghost tale occurred -- the French-Indian war -- the hermit thrush was still not known completely to ornithologists, and certainly not to the chroniclers of the fife-player's tale.

Even scientists were unable to recognize the type of song peculiar to the hermit thrush. Not only obscure in appearance but elusive in its willingness to colonize great expanses of forest, the hermit thrush amounted to a ghost. It remains so to the average person, much like the timber rattlesnake.

That bird song continues the same as it did two centuries ago, and in many ways, so does Cherry Ridge.

This hike proves one of the least arduous hikes I have ever taken. The path is wide and well-kept, the footing good. The shade of the forest keeps the temperature comfortable in summer. Here, however, as in other parts of the Susquehannock Trail, the amount of climbing is considerable. The path rises around 700 vertical feet here.

The illustration is from the Oleona, Pennsylvania 7.5-minute topographic quadrangle.

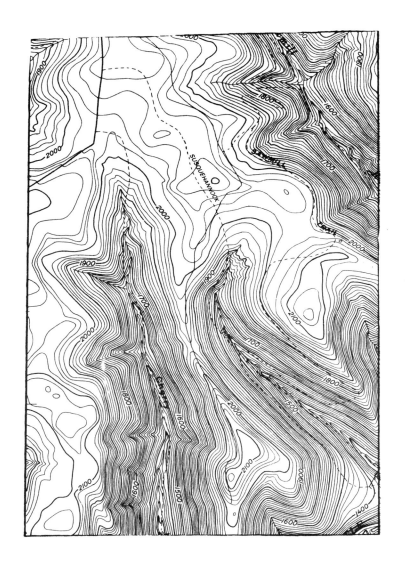

FOXFIRE

Along Route 6 across Pennsylvania's northern counties, Route 44 runs south from the town of Sweden Valley on its way to Carter Camp. Beyond Cherry Springs State Park, it passes over Mount Brodhead.

The road becomes a remote passage through the forest and offers a number of opportunities for pulling off and hiking. The Log Grade Trail passes over the ridge here; in the same vicinity, a pipeline runs off from the road.

The Black Forest of northern Pennsylvania is black not only for its dense trees but its rain and mist that dampen the maple-covered summits for days on end, the crowded treetrunks dark against the fog. I think the rain must be an aspect of inner life there for those natives whose deep eyes and sober looks I have known.

Camped in the Black Forest, the rain falls upon a person, all around him. A black bear walks through the downpour to the edges of the campground as evening settles. The light dims to darkness around the animal and the water pours on its fur, but in complete wildness, it simply walks along.

I lay there on a June night when a lightning flash lit the clearing and the rain pelted down. In the mugginess after the rain, I drifted around and saw lightning lying fallen and still, a flash of lightning on the woodpile. It glowed like the lights of some natural city unto itself, where by day was only broken and sawn wood pieces, fox-orange under the clouds.

It was foxfire, the luminescent fungus, and it came from under the earth, from the roots of a dead sugar maple sapling. It had shown itself on other nights in this clearing, over the years, from diffuse sources: luminous chips from an ax-blasted stump; beneath papery bark, glowing within the rotted heart of a yellow birch limb.

On the high ridges, occupied by millions upon millions of trees, sugar maples and oaks die every day. These maple ridges of the north and oak ridges of the south house fire within them -- foxfire. In the form of the fungus *Armillaria mellea*, foxfire lives within the wood of those trees nature removes through gypsy moth infestation or icestorm.

More than a mere coating of reflective material, foxfire permeates the wood itself and converts it into light. A person expects any such luminescence encountered amidst the dark forest to be lesser, by degrees, than the artificial light we create for ourselves. Then he sees it glowing on the ground, adequate as the light from our batteries, and realizes that it glows for hundreds of miles along the Appalachians.

FOXFIRE

An oak tree weakened by Armillaria fungus topples over and lies uprooted, the old wood of the roots extending into the air. Laid bare, the root system glows with foxfire, large as a human being. A ghost tale arises.

Foxfire occurs often on Brodhead Ridge because sugar maple, a favorite tree for the fungus, covers that ridge. Other regions prove less favorable: the Allegheny National Forest, dominated by black cherry; the high mountains of the Blue Ridge Parkway, covered by spruce and fir.

The rain poured down for days, the foxfire glowed, and a humble world stirred. The rain displaced the self-conscious with the resourceful and carefree, an orange newt crawling over the sogginess from some unsuspected residence.

One day, I walked through the wetness and entered the trees, the enclosed and tranquil chamber that the foxfire inhabited. In the dark woods that held this fungus, the green light of ferns brightened the ground and offered not a drenching but only damp softness to my ankles.

In the Black Forest, "going into the woods" is a statement of living and the forest a provider of rest and comfort from the most stormy or unmanageable circumstances of climate. Hermit thrushes, veeries, ovenbirds, slate-colored juncos all nested on the leafy earth, assured that the roof of tree limbs would keep the rain from washing their young away.

107

Amid the undisciplined lines of the forest floor was a pattern of spots, and the eyes of a fawn. Its mother had conducted a diligent search for dryness: beneath evergreens, under a dead branch of pine here where foxfire lived.

Walking through this forest, drawing together its elements, I made my home in a natural city of life. Here, where foxfire lived, I could break off dead conifer branches for rainy-weather kindling, or gather strips of dusty bark from the down-facing surfaces of leaning birch stubs--a skill of rain culture--or shield the campfire with slabs of flagstone from under the earth, where foxfire and orange newts came from. I could keep my wood dry and have fire in the rain.

Prepare for dampness when hiking here. Often, drizzle persists, offering little fair weather before the approach of further rain or thunder. Otherwise, the hike proves pleasant, among ferns and a forest of straight trees with branch-free trunks.

The illustration is from the Cherry Springs, Pennsylvania 7.5-minute topographic quadrangle.

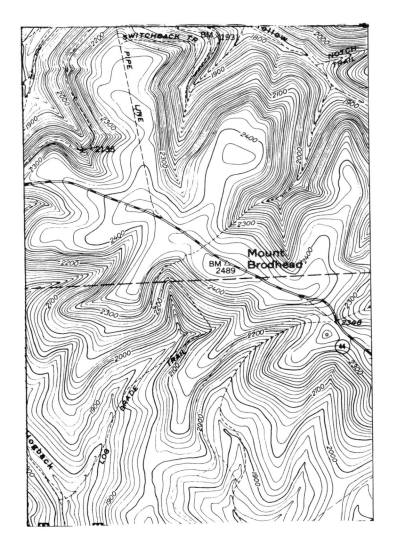

QUARTZ

Humpback Ridge, at milepost 6 of the Blue Ridge Parkway, features a convenient parking area at its base, complete with picnic facilities. The trail leads past a meadow, then continues ascending into hardwood forest until, a mile later, it reaches Humpback Rocks.

East of the Alleghenies, ridges such as Humpback become points of reference, rising thousands of feet above the terrain surrounding them. These ridges are products of a stress that extends from the depths of the earth to where starlight shines on them, stress that began long ago and continues to this point in time. One of the elements of Tuscarora sandstone, quartz, is brought out on its own, in pure form, and forced to sustain this topography in the face of the elements.

Quartz lies on Catoctin Mountain in Maryland, rolling down the mountainside in boulders broken away from large veins of white rock. It lies on Mount Mitchell, the highest ridge in the East, where it is fractured by erosion, amidst the spruce trees, colored like old snow. It stands there at the Pole Steeple, in Pennsylvania's Pine Grove Furnace State Park, a ridgetop formed from sandstone pressed at high temperatures into a closer-grained rock, quartzite.

At Humpback Rocks, a stone wall bordering a meadow shows how the ridges bring rocks and people together. Woods roads near the Parkway in this area further illustrate the relationship with piles of rocks cast up on their sides by the Blue Ridge farmers clearing them.

Sitting atop Humpback Rocks, on Humpback Ridge, I found myself atop a formation of volcanic greenstone. I glanced down and saw white quartz embedded in it. The context in which such quartz lies shows the stress of the Blue Ridge, rising up from within the earth and lying closest to the universe. The greenstone of Humpback Rocks represents basalt from a volcanic flow recrystallized by the pressure of overlying rock.

On this ridge, and in the area of the Parkway between its inception and milepost 40, quartz appears in unusual roles. Twenty miles along, on a peak at the head of the Tye River, it lay pressed as tiny particles of a bluish color, within granite. Fifteen miles further on, beside a woods road, it ran in white streaks amidst brown metabasalt or metarhyolite, products of the metamorphism that created these ridges.

Such granite as occurred above the Tye River is an igneous rock known as charnockite granite comprised of pink feldspar and of epidote, a green mineral formed from the altering of greenstone by the elements. The streaks of quartz within the brown rock further along the Parkway represented molten silica flowing into place and cooling into quartz.

Beneath the oaks on a Blue Ridge crest in North Carolina, I picked up a piece of gneiss. It was sooty-gray with a wood-like grain running across it, producing the fuzzy sensation of trailing arbutus leaves. This grain was quartz.

As the Blue Ridge rises to its highest, in North Carolina, quartz appears within a white granite known as pegmatite. This quartz is gray in color, set amidst white feldspar and pieces of mica.

Much as the highest crests bring the singular orange color to azalea blossoms, they bring unique colors to rocks. Within an hour of cracking pegmatite granite with a hammer, I found a dark crystal, a garnet, wedged within mica. It glowed red in the light. A pink surface, like a pokeberry stain on snow, appeared amidst the white -- a mineral known as thulite, luminescent in black light. The flakes of mica glittered like ice in moonlight.

Inanimate in nature, rocks generally exist without laws protecting them, though certain public lands, including the Parkway, forbid their gathering.

I recently transported a number of quartz boulders home, which I broke into fragments for landscaping. I did it out of aesthetic motivation, as well as the appearance of permanence the rocks provided. I also did it as a reaction to our degree of removal from nature, evidenced in single, gray rocks sold for $10 each at a landscaping store. I was also following long-standing precedent. Throughout the northern Blue Ridges, quartz rocks decorate the crests of stone walls.

I make an effort to select rocks of unusual attractiveness, because they tend to lose their appeal after removal from their point of discovery. Yet, even the most common possess notable properties: crystal, rose-pink or tawny-orange sections of quartz boulders, the sparkle of sandstone.

The emphasis on recreational walking has brought hundreds of trails to the Blue Ridge. The erosive action of footfalls on the ground reveals rocks, together with unintended insight into the geology of these ridges. The erosion of the centuries brought the rock to the surface in the first place. Eroding from the top down, ridges bear a relationship to rock, because generally, only ridges allow us to see rock.

The finest rock I ever found lay exposed by hiking feet at a ridgetop picnic site. I noticed a fragment lying on the ground and found it a lichen-green color, unlike the color of any rock I had known. Continued examination brought out areas of azalea-pink feldspar. In the background, crystals of bluish quartz stood. Its colors elevated it to an aesthetic element, rather than the backdrop that rocks generally constitute. A heavy boulder of it lay there.

I knew the rock as charnockite granite, but I later heard a substantially similar rock referred to as unakite, and saw it in jewelry, polished. Presented in such a way, it represents a piece of the ridge, much as a carving of birch would.

On a spruce ridge near Mount Mitchell, I approached the crest of a path, picking up a glittering chunk of mica schist dislodged by a hiker. At the peak, a gathering of rock provided a resting place amidst the rhododendron. To one side of the path, a slab of rock slanted, offering a weather-protected surface. Initials carved with a chisel in the nineteenth century stood there in the rock. Six thousand feet above the ocean, clouds blew around me.

The trail to Humpback Rocks represents one of a limited number of ridges in that area accessible during all seasons. Though it might appear crowded in the warm months, a walk there in winter offers solitude.

The illustration is from the Sherando, Virginia 7.5-minute topographic quadrangle.

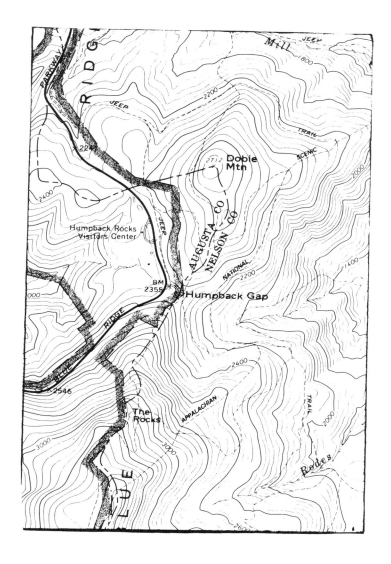

TUSCARORA SANDSTONE

To reach Spruce Ridge, drive south on Route 81 to Route 33, near Harrisonburg, Virginia. About 50 miles along Route 33, beyond the town of Franklin, West Virginia, a National Forest sign announces Spruce Knob, 12 miles up a dirt road. Continue to a paved area around a tourist observation tower.

It becomes immediately apparent that Tuscarora sandstone rocks represent the major resource of this ridge. Along a short path around the observation tower, benches for hikers are fashioned from rocks balanced upon one another. A heap of rock dominates an opening among the spruces. Sandstone comprises the observation tower.

Adjacent to the paved area, the Huckleberry Trail begins, running for several miles along the crest among huckleberry, spruce and rock and then linking up with the Allegheny Mountain Trail, which carries on the ridgetop hiking. Around 10 miles of trail run through here.

The ridgetops constitute the most elemental of environments. There, more than in any other location, a person becomes familiar with the underlying geology of an area, learning something of man's relationship to the earth. On the ridges the

116

elements attack the earth aggressively, exposing rocks to erosion,
allowing the strongest of them to lay in our path as we walk there
through the centuries.

Though Tuscarora sandstone defines the high mountains of
West Virginia more so than rocks anywhere else in the mid-
Atlantic, another type of sandstone impressed me many years ago
while camping in the Allegheny National Forest of northwestern
Pennsylvania. There, arrangements of monstrous rocks, sometimes
40 feet tall and 100 feet long, crown the high places. Yellow birch
trees grow atop them, polypody ferns. Like landscape ornaments,
they rest in the dappled shade of an orderly hardwood forest, the
trees alike in size, on flat ground covered with ferns. They are
called Pocono sandstones.

These rocks represent broken cliffs that once occupied
these peaks in the landscape. Frost and erosion split them and
wore their edges into graceful curves. Many remain close to each
other, one on each side of a hiker's outstretched arms. The shelter
of their faces creates windless settings that invite construction of a
home or camp were the land not federally owned. The even form
of the sides would allow the rock itself to become the wall of a
structure.

Recognizing the impossibility of owning them, we climb
these rocks. At the top, the erosion continues, pink and white
quartz pebbles lying there in the pure air--or grains of sand.

One cold day in April, I climbed above Spring Creek, one of the major watersheds in the Allegheny National Forest. On top of a Pocono sandstone, initials stood chiseled in the rock. Below me, amidst a congregation of the huge rocks, a pit opened up.

Two rocks stood close together, the space between them narrowing into a crevice, at the end of which stood a pot-bellied stove that, 70 years ago, had burnt away the cold in this windless spot.

The people who carved those initials on the rock had crushed this sandstone, loaded the sand that resulted into containers that they transported off of the ridge. At the base of the slope had stood a glass factory.

I looked across the valley at Wolf Creek and the huge sandstones above it. I knew that timber wolves, when they inhabited the Allegheny National Forest, preferred rocks in which to den. I also knew that Wolf Creek received its name for a reason.

On Hawk mountain, in eastern Pennsylvania, sandstone boulders crowd the ridge. An operation similar to this one produced glass at the turn of the century.

In the midst of the Appalachian mountains, in the Alleghenies, soil again gives way to rock, though rock of a different pattern. On these ridges, stone piles upon stone in a kind of rock garden, pale in tone as if bleached.

The type of rock differs as well. Rather than the pink pebbles of quartz atop the Pocono sandstones, chunks of pink sandstone lie about. White sandstone lies there with it. A decorative variety, creamy-white infused with tawny-orange and pink, is common. We call them Tuscarora sandstones.

Tuscarora sandstone is a tightly cemented type of sandstone known for its resistance to weathering. Its appearance suggests marble, quartz, rather than sandstone. Then, too, rather than lying in flat slabs, it lies in chunks and fragments.

The existence of Tuscarora sandstone on the crests, curious to the person who associates sand with low places, illustrates the creation of these ridges. They began as deposits of sand and became a ridge when thrust upward by the forces that created the high places.

On ridgetops from central New Jersey, through the Delaware Water Gap and southward all the way to Alabama, hiking boots fall on Tuscarora sandstone. This rock comprises high points of topography along the ridges running immediately west of the Blue Ridge mountains such as Massanutten Mountain. Tuscarora sandstone lying on these ridges is over 400 million years old.

Originating in a portion of geologic time known as the Silurian period, this sandstone not only formed the outlines of the mountains but opened up with the eroding force of water, allowing the course of present-day rivers to take shape. It therefore oversaw the colonization of America as the earliest settlers followed the waterways, pursuing agriculture, building cities.

Though susceptible to erosion on such a long-term scale, this stone tends to defeat small-scale efforts to wear it down. Certain sandstones prove compatible with man as sources of sand, such as Pocono sandstone. The hardness of Tuscarora sandstone makes it more resistant to such processes.

Tuscarora sandstone found its greatest utility at the height of the Industrial Revolution. In the 1920s, it was crushed and, in combination with sand and refractory clays, lined the ladles used in steel-making operations. Its value in such a role came from its low iron content, which prevented its melting under heat. This quality allowed it to act as a barrier to impurities that might pass within products.

Tuscarora sandstone, in the form of bricks consisting of clay, sand and the crushed stone itself, constituted the lining of glass furnaces and coke ovens. As a component of brick, it found its most widespread use. This use continued to modern times, until the process involved in steel-making changed to require fewer heating and cooling cycles and the heat-absorbing qualities of the Tuscarora bricks lost their importance.

The same hardness that positions this rock in the face of the ridgetop elements makes it more difficult to blast from the ground and gives it the tendency to wear out equipment used in handling it. As a result, production has dropped to perhaps 100, 000 pounds per year, very minor in commercial terms. A prospective use involves appropriating its hardness as an ingredient of road surfaces, where the resistant fragments would reduce skidding.

Short-term economics overlook the highest use of this stone -- as shelter. Cut into blocks, it forms enduring structures free of maintenance considerations. This use exists today on a scale that makes it more commemorative than functional, however.

On the crest near Huntingdon, Pennsylvania, a gap in the topography indicates an old quarry of Tuscarora sandstone dating from the time when this stone accompanied our pursuit of progress. The empty spaces of such lost quarries represent the loss of nature's prone face meeting the sun and wind on the ridges.

Lichens accompany much of the rock on the ridges. They cling to them as though, in doing so, they will acquire the same unchanging nature as the stone itself -- and as the ridges, the most enduring and resistant setting in the eastern mountains.

Though no-one blocks the road to Spruce Ridge after October, the weather proves forbidding, the elevation bringing snow and ice. Even in the warm months, the mountain climate brings chills.

The Huckleberry Trail, though running over a rock-strewn area, offers fair footing on the path itself. On a summer day, it offers a pleasant walk over the highest ground in the Allegheny Mountains.

The illustration is from the Spruce Knob, West Virginia 7.5-minute topographic quadrangle.

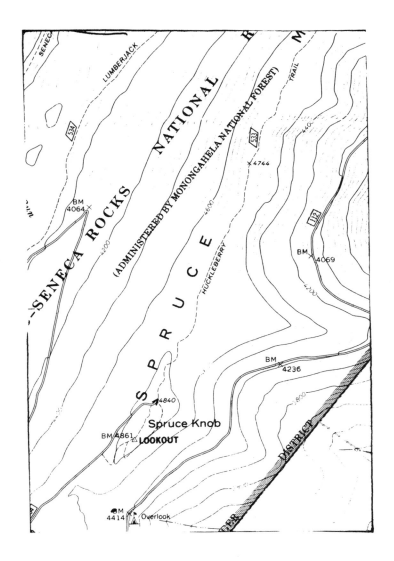

BEAR TRAIL

At milepost 349.2 on the Blue Ridge Parkway, a pull-off affords one of the outstanding views from that scenic road. A glance at the nearby terrain also makes it apparent that the land here reaches a peak of ruggedness.

Crowding the Parkway on the east side is a slope rising several hundred feet. In order to reach it, walk a short distance south on the Parkway and enter the woods where the angle of slope lessens. Then begin climbing to the top to view perhaps the most rugged piece of ground within the Blue Ridge Mountain chain.

As the Blue Ridge Mountains extend southward, the crests of the ridges lift upward until, rather than standing 500 or 600 feet above their surroundings, they stand 3000 feet, 4000 feet.

Almost a mile above the valley, rising atop rock and covered with forest, the ridgetop represents the inmost recess of a vertical wilderness. It constitutes a refuge reaching not inward but upward, and at its peak near the sky, plants and animals become glamorous in appearance and dramatic in form.

Within the deepest part of this wilderness, the weather becomes singular in its operations. One afternoon, a spring afternoon lit with the brightness of the south, I passed over a section of the Parkway known as Thunder Ridge. Only a few yards of road revealed itself as I went, because mist shrouded the ridge, and blew over the ridge as well, owing to its height, which brought it into contact with the wind currents.

Out of the whiteness came the sound of thunder, from where I couldn't tell -- at the spot over which I walked, I supposed, since I was within a cloud. The wind blew cold, yet thunder rumbled. The thunder accompanied me, rather than existing within the detached perspective one is accustomed to.

Here, the Blue Ridge becomes a definition of ridgetops, extending for hundreds of miles, and whereas much of the life of the ridge in general could be termed typical of ridges, yet not unknown in other locations, here, certain species become basically limited to the ridgetop environment.

Not content with the delicate pink of wild azaleas, the ridgetop here offers us an orange azalea, flame azalea, which, with its color of a summer sun setting, gives us the color of July in a May blossom. The flowers are a celebration of southern sunshine. On the ridge, the sunlight reaches the shrubs unimpeded by the shadows of slopes.

Amidst the chestnut oaks and boulders around Humpback Rocks, at 3000 feet some 140 miles south of Front Royal , Virginia, I took note of the northernmost flame azaleas in the vicinity of the Blue Ridge Parkway. The environment around them was cool, rich in plant life, situated amidst increasing moisture as the Blue Ridge runs south, yet stronger sun as well.

Distorted in form by the winds of the crestline, an unusual variety of northern red oak colonizes the ridge at certain points along the Blue Ridge Parkway. The ridgetop gives this variety of tree its existence. In other habitats, it is absent.

Reaching the heart of this wilderness of height, the trees become dense. No-one has logged these woods. Rather than growing upward and producing lengths of lumber, the trees spread out and run together. On the mountaintop, up to 80 inches of rain falls each year, nurturing their growth. They produce acorns and provide shelter.

Mountain laurel sometimes reaches three feet in circumference in the Blue Ridges -- a small tree rather than a shrub, its status among woodland plants enhanced by the tough leaves and durable qualities that serve it well at higher elevations.

Within this thick growth, black bears range about. In the Blue Ridge, the black bear becomes a creature of the ridgetops, enough so that motorists driving the Parkway spot them crossing. Though the black bear today finds the ridge a convenient setting for the defensive lifestyle that colonization has forced upon him, this animal by its nature retreats to the dense oaks and rhododendrons of the ridgetop when threatened.

Here on Rough Ridge, in North Carolina, rhododendrons stand close together, so close that a person works through them and rests in an open place with no thought of traveling on. Though views open upon either side, the branches block them. A mountain pine (*Pinus pungens*), much like a pitch pine but possessed of sharper-edged and larger cones, along with the willingness to colonize the high places, stands up above the shrubs.

Standing on the crest of Rough Ridge, Beth indicated her relief that a trail ran through the rhododendron. Indeed, a path running there spoke of a definite presence. It was a bear trail.

Like many ridges, Rough Ridge constitutes a boundary. It marks the Tennessee Valley Divide, the boundary of Yancey and McDowell Counties, North Carolina, and that of Blue Ridge Parkway-owned land.

This hike, without the benefit of a marked path, nevertheless provides a safe walk. The sound of the Parkway below serves as a compass and a reminder that the car sits only a few hundred yards away. Yet, the thickets prove daunting. To hike Rough Ridge, devote several hours to that purpose and move slowly and deliberately, working with the environment rather than against it. I recommend it in June, when the pink rhododendron on the crest are in bloom.

The illustration is from the Old Fort, North Carolina 7.5-minute topographic quadrangle.

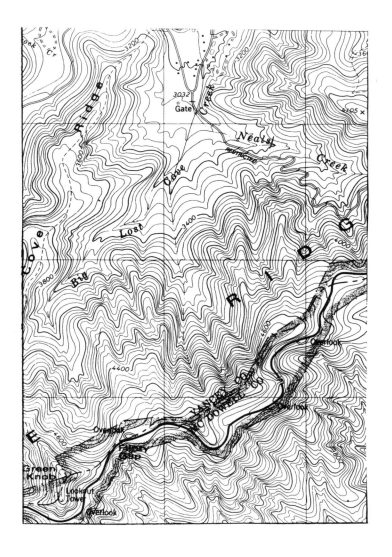

HIGHER GROUND

At milepost 354.9 on the Blue Ridge Parkway, a gate stands on the north side of the road. Park there, being careful not to block it. Behind the gate, the trail begins as a woods road and then ascends into conifer forest before changing abruptly into a rough path scratching to the crest of the ridge.

This path marks a change in mountain ranges from the Blue Ridges to the Black Mountains The habitat through which it runs reflects the name, given in recognition of the dark evergreen trees in this range. At the same time, it serves to divide Yancey and Buncombe Counties, North Carolina, as well as the properties of the Blue Ridge Parkway, public ground; and the Asheville Watershed, private property.

A person climbing to the very crest of the Appalachian mountains reaches the utmost recess of their wildness in hiking in the Black Mountain range. I noticed the intensity of the forest growth increasing. I felt as though I should abandon my steps and sit down. Upon doing so, I found in the high tangles a certain softness, a declaration of life's value expressed as its defense from the sky around it up there.

Like snow, a softness settles on the branches and logs.
Cledonia lichen covers the smallest twigs in places unbroken by
the arms and legs of hikers. Puffs of cotton moss cling to
treetrunks. Moss covers the fallen spruce logs, which comprise a
second layer of matter so dense it nearly covers the ground. The
fresh green of new Carolina hemlock needles lies on the drooping
branches like gentle flakes. Through the spruce boughs is the soft
whiteness of surrounding clouds. The earth is covering its strife,
holding secrets beneath softness.

The evergreen trunks of red spruce rise perfectly straight,
with an elemental form as simple as the form of the white clouds
filling the spaces between them. On the ridge, I learn that trees are
meant to be straight.

Yet, I have had to come to the highest mountains to learn
this. A nation that has destroyed its virgin forest has forced us to
do so. I find here that my feet are meant for a soft surface. Moss
lies here like a cushion. In open stretches of spruce woods, grass
covers the earth. Here, at the closest point in the east to the sky, I
am reminded that the life that has made our paths hard and altered
the treetrunks into crookedness exists below us -- at a lower level.

Beneath the wind blowing at a steady 30 knots, the rushing
clouds, ridgetop life hides in softness. A painted trillium, white
with a heart of bright pink like the brightness of the
rhododendrons, grows here, as it does on many crests. Hay-

scented fern and wood sorrel grow in openings between the spruces.

The land here no longer represents a garden of various tree species. The trees that remain here are elements of ruggedness. An occasional mountain ash appears, a scattered fire cherry, a witch-hobble or two -- all abbreviated.

In places on the ridge, patches of domestic ease appear in the form of small lawns of grass within the rhododendrons. They are referred to as balds. Sphagnum moss covers the ground there, as if from a long-lost bog.

Fraser fir, a decorative conifer perhaps 40 feet tall, grows on the highest of these ridges. Rhododendron, not the white species of Pennsylvania but a red species and a pink species, covers the ground.

The softness is held in permanence by the fullness of the evergreen branches. Within them are birds of the north such as the pine siskin, generally seen as a migrating bird in the remaining conifers of the east, but remaining here year-round. Here, it bursts forth from the tangles with an intricate song.

Here, where the earth and sky come closest, as the wind swirls about, the earth holds itself in a silence enhanced by the stillness of needles, twigs, mosses, sticks crowded together. A raindrop slips from the moss covering a spruce trunk. It is clear as quartz. In the wetness, a red leaf of emerging galax shines like a berry.

When hiking on Pinnacle Ridge, dress warmly and dress for rain. Mist obscures the surroundings and makes it advisable to hike with a partner. Remain on the trails, because the ground surrounding them proves rugged -- blowdowns, dense conifer growth, gaps between rocks invite injury, especially to an individual lost and hurried.

The illustration is from the Montreat, North Carolina 7.5-minute topographic quadrangle.

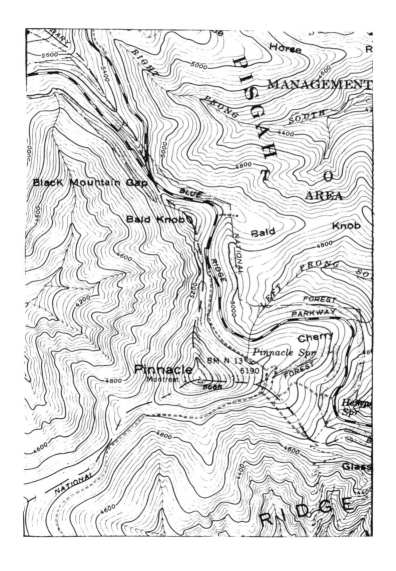

BLACK MOUNTAINS

At milepost 359.9 on the Blue Ridge Parkway in North Carolina, a small parking area on the right side of the road traveling south marks entry to the Mountains-to-Sea hiking trail. To the right, the trail climbs through the forest, following switchbacks to a ridgecrest atop the Black Mountains. Its elevation, along with the fact that it connects to Mount Mitchell, 6684 feet, make this the defining ridgetop hike in the east.

Black Ridge, like much of the Black Mountains, is an abstract place. There, above all other high points in the east, the world becomes less a place of specific names and more one of symbols.

Along this trail, great birch trees stand. Their trunks, misshapen, reach up to four feet across, large enough to hide behind, their bark an indistinct covering. They offer nothing that identifies them as either yellow birch or black birch. Age and size eliminate the distinctions.

Early lumbermen no doubt encountered the same appearance and simply cut such trees as birch lumber. These trees, however, grew on the ridge and were limited in height due to poor conditions. The lumbermen looked at them and decided they possessed no value as lumber as squat trees 40 or 50 feet tall. Hundreds of years old, they memorialize the forest as they finally die of age.

Bracket funguses find their old trunks. Unconstrained by the contrived intervals of growth created by lumbering, they offer nature's history, indicating the trees' demise as they grow there and, through their layered pattern, providing markers showing the years that pass.

As these birches represent defining birches of America, so a small conifer on this stretch of trail represents our defining conifer. It grows high on the Black Mountain ridges -- Fraser Fir.

Like those birches, many Fraser Firs stood virgin on the ridge. They remained untouched because the species attains a height much less than that of the red spruce with which it associates. Along this trail, red spruce rises up 100 feet above the path, trunks three feet through and straight as columns.

The Fraser Fir (*A. fraseri*) stands 30 or 40 feet tall, with the cone-shaped outline our mind associates with conifers. The boughs fill in that outline fully with needles larger than those of red spruce, whitened beneath. Small cones stand upright on them rather than drooping downward as the spruce cones do. To a greater extent than spruce needles, Fraser Fir needles persist on their boughs after cutting, contributing to the species' value as a Christmas tree. A twig in my desk drawer holds onto brittle needles after five months.

Such qualities contribute to the tree's status as a Christmas symbol, grown by the thousands throughout the region. Other than these fine points, this is not a tree of distinctive botanical characteristics, but a tree of notable qualities, rather.

On the ridge, the death of an entire species is evidently taking place in the disappearance of the Fraser Fir. At this point, mature trees prove difficult to find in the forest. In a short time, they may vanish entirely. Their demise is moving forth in solitude, without our understanding of it.

We know that balsam wooly aphids attack Fraser Firs. Yet, with a species millions of years old, not the prime object of the turn-of-the-century lumbering industry, its disappearance from the ridge presents an event embedded in ages. That human beings, a few centuries of life amidst millions-year-old rocks, should witness this is notable.

The balsam wooly aphid originated in Europe. Around 40 years ago, it appeared in this region and began its destruction of the Fraser Fir. It lives by sucking the sap from the trunks.

A Christmas symbol dies. We focus public speculation on this fir as a species. Some blame acid rain in combination with the aphid. Perhaps the desire to reach the ridgetop, the exhaust from cars on the Parkway, contributes. Perhaps global warming shifted the temperature to the extent of destroying the environmental balance the tree demands. Like the birches along this trail, the firs die of their own accord, beyond man's designs on them.

HIGH GROUND

Walking the Mountains-to-Sea Trail, a hiker finds that it transcends the outdoor museum that many trails below represent. Here, as much as bark identification, there is wind. It sighs through the conifers. There are clouds running through the green boughs. Virgin birches never cut, a species of tree vanishing, tell us that understanding takes us no further.

This trail proves easy to hike, with conifer needles underfoot and an ascent of the mountainside involving switchbacks rather than a straight climb. On the left side of the Parkway traveling south, the trail continues.

The section on Black Mountain Ridge marks the border of Pisgah National Forest, as well as that of Yancey and Buncombe Counties, North Carolina.

Climate offers the greatest challenge here. Frequently, clouds run across the Parkway, obscuring the turnoff for the parking lot; in the woods, they reduce the hike to a study of treetrunks and evergreen boughs amidst fog. The dark spruce-fir forest takes away the light from the forest floor early in the evening, making the trail easy to lose once a person leaves it briefly.

The illustration is from the Montreat, North Carolina 7.5-minute topographic quadrangle.

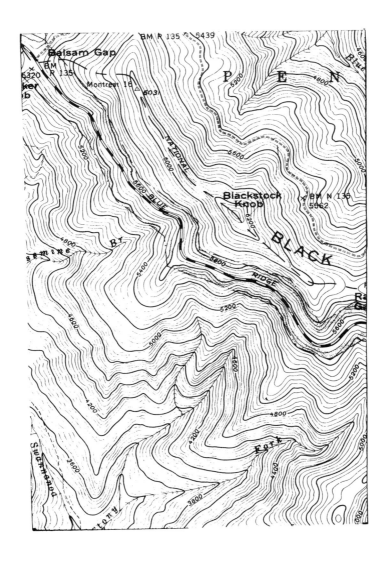

INDEX

INDEX